KATHY FISCUS

A Tragedy That Transfixed The Nation

KATHY FISCUS

A Tragedy That Transfixed The Nation

William Deverell

ANGEL CITY PRESS

For Helen and John

Fiscus, Katherine [sic]
A call was received by this dept. that the above had fallen in a hole.

San Marino Police Department
Desk Officer Bliss
April 8, 1949

Introduction

HOW MANY TIMES have I thought of the moment when idle banter between two sisters, both mothers of small children, turned to confused silence, then concern, then fear? Hundreds, easily, probably thousands. I have wondered over and over again what Alice Fiscus said to her sister as the sun cast its waning light across that little kitchen. "Where did Kathy go?" "Where's Kathy?" "Now where has Kathy run off to?"

What is it about this story that I cannot shake? It is a type of haunting. A few years ago, I was talking about Kathy Fiscus with my dear friend and fellow historian David Igler. "You are going to have to write that book, you know," he said. It was a matter-of-fact observation. Even a directive. He was right.

As a historian, my job is to try to assemble the fragile, fragmentary puzzle pieces of the past. Establish chronology, narrate change, assess cause and effect: bring the past into conversation with the present. This is what historians do as teachers and writers. It is endlessly fascinating—a strange, heady mix of expertise and fool's errand. I have never doubted that I found what I was meant to do. I have never worked on a project that has occupied my thoughts or my dreams in any way close to the way this story has.

I can walk from my home to the area where Alice Fiscus stood in the kitchen chatting with her sister Jeanette on that late afternoon of April 8, 1949. The landscape is changed now. But with luck, a good map, and a historic photograph, I can get within ten feet of where Alice looked out that window and first realized that her youngest child had disappeared. I have tried it before, and I feel like trying it again as I write this.

Proximity surely has something to do with this story's hold on me. I am a historian of the American West and especially of California. This is fundamentally a California story, although it very quickly reverberated across the nation and the world. Its Californianess feels very close to me, and to what I think and write about in my work. There is also proximity by way of chronology. I tend to work in the nineteenth and twentieth centuries. Those hundred years between the Civil War and my birth in 1962 feel familiar. I spend a lot of time contemplating them.

Compared to most of my work, this episode feels nearly contemporary; 1949 is only thirteen years before I was born. I know plenty of people born well before 1949. It just wasn't that long ago. The sheer closeness of the events in this story, in both time and place, is part of what intrigues me.

But who am I kidding? "Intrigues me" is not the half of it. This story obsesses me. The roots and persistence of that obsession raise questions that I cannot easily answer.

Fatherhood is part of it. My wife and I have two children. Our son, John, is in high school. Our daughter, Helen, is a university student. They are young adults, but I still worry about their safety as they venture out and about—driving, cycling, camping, rock climbing—just being who they are and doing what they do.

On a weekend afternoon more than a decade ago, I asked my daughter, who was seven or eight at the time, if she would help me with a project. Could she cut a circle from a sheet of construction paper? Helen said yes. She liked craft projects with paper and scissors. I told her that the circle needed to be fourteen inches in diameter, and I held my hands that far apart.

Helen went out back to the playroom and returned with a sheaf of construction paper. She sat on the floor of our living room, right by the big front window. She tore out a purple piece of paper and quickly figured out how to complete her task, maybe with a little help. She marked two cardinal points on the paper north and south, fourteen inches apart. Then two more, east and west, likewise fourteen inches apart. With a pen, she drew a circle connecting all four points. She then carefully cut the circle from the paper and held it up. "Like this?"

I remember the moment as if it were yesterday. From where I write this, I can look to our living room where Helen proudly held up the purple circle in the light of that big window. I caught my breath. It is one thing to know how small fourteen inches is. It is something else entirely to see it, especially once we had taped it to the hardwood floor. The circle is the shape and diameter of the old well that three-year-old Kathy Fiscus fell into late that April afternoon in 1949.

A tube of rusted metal, just over a foot in diameter. A circle of purple construction paper a lifetime later. Now this little book, long in the making.

Barbara and Kathy Fiscus.

Chapter 1

FRIDAY, APRIL 8, 1949, arrived cool and breezy in Southern California. Sometime that morning, Alice Fiscus put her two girls in the family car and drove to Union Station in downtown Los Angeles to pick up her sister Jeanette Lyon, Jeanette's husband Hamilton, and their two boys. The Lyons had traveled up from Chula Vista, near San Diego, to spend the weekend in San Marino so their children, close in age, could play. The Fiscus girls, Barbara ("Babs") and Kathy, were nine and three. Their Lyon cousins, Stanley and Gus, were ten and five.

Alice Fiscus was recovering from some recent surgery. Her doctor insisted that, as she recuperated, she was not to pick up or hold Kathy. But at the big train station, something startled the little girl—maybe the bustling crowd, or a train whistle, or the rumble of an engine—and Kathy jumped into her mother's arms. For the first time in six months, Alice stood and held her youngest child. Kathy stayed in Alice's arms most of the time at the train station. "I always felt that I was so glad . . . to have had the opportunity to do that," Alice would later say.[1]

Alice, Jeanette, Hamilton, and the children all piled into the Fiscus's Studebaker and drove home on the Arroyo Seco Parkway. Back at home in San Marino, about a dozen miles northeast of downtown, Alice caught up with her sister. By late afternoon, the

The field behind the Fiscus home.

Kathy Fiscus

kids had gone out behind the house to play in a big and weedy six-acre field. The family's beloved brown-and-white terrier, Jeepers, romped alongside.

Alice and Jeanette began to prepare dinner, visiting as they did. Alice stood at her kitchen window where she could look out onto the field. The cousins got along well. While their mothers chatted, they ran and played. It was nearing four-thirty, and the sun began its dip toward sunset. "I could see the kids out back playing," Alice said. "Just running, as children do."[2] She heard them laugh as they played. Jeepers ran back and forth with them, excited to have so many playmates. Kathy lagged behind the other children, still in the pink party dress she had worn to the train station. They would look back. She would catch up, and then quickly fall behind again.

Alice counted heads. Three, not four. The littlest child was missing. She was just there. Now she was not. Where had she gone?

She went out back and asked the children where Kathy had gone. The others thought she was hiding. Maybe she was angry with the bigger kids for racing ahead of her. Or perhaps she had gone over to the new playground at the K.L. Carver Elementary School at the far end of the field. Alice sensed that something was wrong. She got into the Studebaker and drove over to the school-yard. Not finding Kathy, she came right back and went out to the field again.

Gus Lyon heard cries near a tractor in the field. He went to investigate. "She's here!" he shouted. It was Kathy. Alice would later say it was "an absolute miracle" that Gus heard her.

Kathy had fallen into a well.[3]

Chapter 2

A CHILD IN HARM'S WAY: a story as old as humanity. Each event is different in innumerable facets, each episode reverberating through time and space, family, and community. So it is with Kathy. The Kathy Fiscus story has a concentric geometry. At the very center is an abandoned well and its circle of a mouth, hiding in a weedy field. From there, radiating out in time and space, we find family members crouched in stunned fear around that opening, once Gus Lyon shouted that he had found his missing cousin. Then more and more people arrived, hours ticking by, a couple of days come and gone; thousands eventually gathered near that little well mouth. And the story travelled beyond, far beyond. News stories sent round the world, the fate of the little girl unknown, people praying, weeping, some offering ideas as to how to get Kathy out of the well, others coming to the scene offering to help.

This incident, a little girl fallen down an old well, transcends melodrama—the Kathy Fiscus episode changed lives and changed culture. Every moment would reveal so much in the details, just as each would reveal broader truths beyond the central thread of a child in danger. Certainly, the Fiscus family was never the same again, nor were the lives of others brought urgently and intimately into the story as it unspooled over time. But the reverberations and legacies extend beyond that. The Kathy Fiscus event changed

The Fiscus home.

Kathy Fiscus

journalism forever. It is one of the most significant events in the history of television media. It changed the lives of families in the United States and beyond who could not, or chose not to, shake free of the event's impact on how they loved, protected, and even named their children.

The primary story begins and ends at the old well. But to get there, to arrive in that field on that pretty spring day, we must first move toward that spot across natural and human histories. Seismology, geology, and hydrology all have a role to play. Natural histories that extend beyond human history—as they always do—affect how people act, how they live, and how they come together, converging on that narrow metal pipe on a Friday afternoon in April 1949.

Chapter 3

IN THE SUMMER OF 1903, a man named C.C. Johnson drilled a well deep into the big aquifer below San Marino. It was 603 feet above sea level, 572 feet south of Robles Avenue, and 172 feet west of Santa Anita Avenue. The metal casing of the Johnson Well was fourteen inches in diameter for the first 507 feet. From that point, the casing narrowed to ten inches until it reached 784 feet below the earth's surface. As Johnson's drill went down, it penetrated the different strata of the earth. Every ten to twenty feet, the sediments changed: soil, gravel, clay, blue clay, cement sand, hard clay.

The cast iron casing would have been perforated—scraped and scratched by cutting tools that opened small gashes—after it had been set into the hole, so that water in the aquifer could seep into the well casing and rise to the earth's surface. Perforations were made in sections: from fifty to ninety feet, for example, or from 128 feet to 152 feet. The perforations would have left the casing with jagged and irregular gashes. If they were careful, the men doing the perforating would only make the gashes where the various soils would not foul the water coming into the pipe. They would have picked their spots to score the metal carefully, based on what they knew about the varying sedimentary layers lying one atop another.

In Southern California, well-digging had become sophisticated by the 1890s. Even so, it was not uncommon to bring dowsing rods to bear in search of water, as agriculturalists and others looked for the best spots to tap into the big supply of water that lay under the surface of the earth. Wells—the Johnson Well among them—went far below where they first encountered water to tap deep into the aquifer, far down into the water table where there was more water and more water pressure.

Wells bored by drills tended to be small in diameter. Same with those excavated by a cable system: a heavy bit was lifted above the earth and then dropped—over and over again—to pulverize the soil and make a deep hole. Though crude, this technique worked well, as the bit tore into the alluvial soils washed down over the millennia from the nearby San Gabriel Mountains. Wells dug with shovels were all shapes and sizes, sunk down into the earth looking for water. There is a surprising diversity to wells if you look at them long enough. No two are alike: no two go into or under the ground the same way, no two travel the same distance into the earth, and no two travel through the same geologic structures or circumstances.

All those wells dug into the Raymond Basin tell stories of community: community formation, community relations, and community sustenance. Benjamin "Don Benito" Wilson, a prominent New Englander who later became a Mexican citizen, was the mid-nineteenth century patron of the region. He owned the Rancho San Pasqual, a huge swath of land that is now taken up by the cities of Pasadena, South Pasadena, San Marino, Alhambra, Altadena, and San Gabriel. Wilson knew the waters of the region. He brought water to his property via an aqueduct known locally as the "Wilson Ditch." He started the first commercial water company of the area in 1875, the Lake Vineyard Land and Water Association, which was purchased by the Alhambra Addition Water Company in 1883.

In 1867, Don Benito's daughter, Maria de Jesus ("Sue"), married a man named James De Barth Shorb. At least for a time, they lived like royalty on a huge 600-acre ranch that Wilson gave them. They named their ranch San Marino, after Shorb's grandfather's plantation in Maryland that, in turn, had taken its name from the tiny European republic.

The name stuck. Shorb developed the property because he knew it had water under it. That knowledge alone was almost enough to ensure success. But not quite; he failed and went broke.[1] Shorb sold the ranch to Henry Huntington in 1903. Huntington had made plans to relocate to Southern California from San Francisco and New York. He had fallen in love with the ranching landscape when he had been a guest of the Shorbs. At the turn of the century, Huntington came into millions upon the death of his uncle, railroad baron Collis P. Huntington. Within a decade, he doubled that largesse into a formidable dynasty when he married Collis Huntington's widow, his aunt Arabella. Through the first three decades of the twentieth century, Huntington monopolized the trolley systems in Southern California, adding more millions to his fortune by way of land development (and making Southern California into the decentralized metropolis it is). He turned much of his money into the greatest book collection ever assembled in American history. The collection, and the art he and his wife acquired, still reside on the San Gabriel Valley property he bought well over a century ago.

Another of Benjamin Wilson's daughters, Ruth, who was Sue Wilson's half-sister, married Huntington's business partner, George Patton. Father to his famed namesake, the World War II

Army general, and indispensable superintendent of much of the operations of rail baron Henry Huntington, the senior George Patton oversaw the digging of several wells for his rich partner in the San Gabriel Valley in the early twentieth century.

As this well-watered part of the San Gabriel Valley grew at the end of the nineteenth century—and answered the agricultural demands of greater Los Angeles and beyond—more wells dove down into the Raymond Basin. That made this part of Southern California one of the most celebrated agricultural regions of the state. With water drawn from the aquifer below, the Johnson Well helped water this fertile landscape. The fields supported a variety of fruit trees: persimmons, peaches, plums, oranges, grapefruit, nectarines, lemons, and apricots.[2]

The San Gabriel Valley grew up around the Johnson Well. Storm drains went under local streets, taking away the water that those springs and little creeks brought from the north to the south. Children who grew up in the area remember sliding into those drains from curbside to play in the damp darkness below or walking far into the old gigantic culverts that emptied water from the vast Huntington property onto the land and streets below the estate's grand perch.

In 1907, the San Gabriel Valley Water Company bought up the Alhambra Addition Water Company's wells, pumps, and pipes, as well as its buildings, its hydrants, and, most important, its water rights. Stock in the San Gabriel Valley Water Company was nearly wholly owned by Henry Huntington's gigantic holding company, the Huntington Land and Improvement Company. George Patton Sr. served as president of the Alhambra Addition Water Company.

The metal-and-concrete web atop and beneath the earth—made

Kathy Fiscus

of wells and pumps, water mains, hydrants, and the pipes—spread across the landscape. Field books of Henry Huntington's holding company reveal all this in engineering taxonomies, drawings, and measurements. In tiny pencil script—written with what must have been a very sharp pencil—engineers took the measure of all that the water regime on this landscape meant and did. These hundreds of field books—leather-bound and easy to hold in the palm—were tools as much as they were books, the equations, measurements, and renderings within them shaping that landscape around the Johnson Well.

Not long after taking over, the new water company spent $182.40 repairing the casing of the Johnson Well. In the field all around the Johnson Well, engineers marked the irrigation landscape (referred to as "good water-bearing lands") in their survey books with their particular nomenclature: flumes, valves, ditches, pipes, wells. Other language is in here, too: an "alfalfa patch" marks a boundary, as does a "seedling orange orchard." At times, the surveyors found relics of the past in their work: a rusty pipe here and there (from earlier well and irrigation work), an old property-line stake. Throughout the 1910s, much attention was paid to the area all around the Johnson Well.

The intersection of Santa Anita and Robles Avenues—so close to where Alice Fiscus would later look out her kitchen window on a late April afternoon—is part of many drawings in these field books. That spot marked an especially wet center of the area, as Johnson certainly knew.[3]

This landscape was not without peril. Building that web of irrigation systems posed dangers to the workers who drilled the wells, dug the ditches, laid the flumes. Those dangers extended beyond the workers, too, and even beyond the years in which those pipes, wells, and drains were in service. George Patton expressed concern over just such danger in a letter he sent up the company chain of command in the summer of 1919. The company owned several of the old tunnels that drained water at the southern end of Henry Huntington's property. These tunnels worried him. Patton had contacted company officers to complain that neighborhood boys played inside these tunnels. That made him "afraid that some of them will get hurt, or that some damage will be done by lawless persons." Patton thought the tunnels to be "a menace to the neighborhood." The water company agreed—it did not need or use these tunnels any longer—and suggested that Huntington's estate manager might "put in a couple of shots of giant powder or dynamite and cave in these entrances enough so that the boys cannot open them up. We have, on several occasions, closed these entrances, but they continue to dig them up."[4] Children, water, pipes, and tunnels: it was all cause for concern.

Just after the First World War, the Johnson Well petered out and became inoperative. It had not been in service long, no more than about fifteen years. Maybe the casing had been damaged or bent, deep down in the earth. It was in earthquake country, after all. Maybe the Raymond Fault shook the Raymond Basin and crunched that pipe below. Or perhaps that portion of the aquifer punctured by the Johnson Well had yielded the water it would provide, at least for a while. Reports filed with the state railroad commission—a precursor agency to California's Public Utilities Commission—show the Johnson Well pulling up just over 23,000 cubic feet of water in 1916. That may seem like a lot, but compared to other wells in service nearby, it was not that much water at all.

In the report filed in 1919, the San Gabriel Valley Water Company lists the Johnson Well as "not in use." Officials may have tried to cap the well, sealing it at the top for safety. That cover may have fallen off, or may have never existed in the first place. We do know that by the spring of 1949, the well was open. It looks to have just sat there, unused, abandoned, and largely forgotten.[5]

In 1929, not long after Henry Huntington's death, the Western Utilities Corporation bought the San Gabriel Valley Water Company. Western Utilities, in turn, was sold in 1935 to the California Water and Telephone Company. The water rights, the well, and the land around it went with everything else.

The abandoned Johnson Well sat forgotten in the field and weeds. Nearby sat an adobe, built in 1845 by an English adventurer named Michael Claringbud White. White, who also went by Miguel Blanco, knew there was water here: spongy land, a pond or two, a wash just to the west, and water below the surface of the earth. His tiny adobe is still there.

The Johnson Well may have stuck up a bit, the casing rising perhaps a few inches from grade level in that field. If there ever was a cap welded on it, or maybe just a metal plate laid across its mouth, it fell off at some point. Or someone yanked it off. Or as the story goes in the neighborhood, it got knocked off by a tractor or other disking machine cutting weeds in that field. Perhaps the machine banged into the well and knocked the cover loose and the operator never put it back. Local lore has it that neighborhood children knew about the well. They liked to throw rocks and other things down it and probably wondered just how far it went down. Weeds grew around the well.

Cap. No cap. No way to know for sure.

Chapter 4

THERE IS A LOT OF WATER under the San Gabriel Valley, home to Pasadena, San Marino, and other Southern California suburban cities and towns. Three underground water basins—the Main San Gabriel Basin, the Raymond Groundwater Basin, and the Puente Basin—act as storage for a tremendous amount of water. The Raymond Groundwater Basin, usually referred to as the Raymond Basin (which is at the center of our story), is a forty-square-mile subterranean geologic feature running on a northeast-to-southwest axis through and under the valley. Its shape and geologic structure allow it to form an aquifer, essentially a catch basin for water that, because it is stored under pressure, can be drawn to the surface by wells. The triangular basin gathers water from streams flowing off the San Gabriel Mountains that rise steeply to the north. The aquifer is made of innumerable seeps of water underneath what is now Huntington Drive, one of the valley's major east/west thoroughfares. These days, about a million and a half people live in the two hundred miles that make up the San Gabriel Valley.

The amount of water above ground in the valley looks modest now. Long ago, springs and marshy land were more common here, but these have long ago disappeared or lie hidden in the nooks and crannies of suburban and urban development. But hundreds of thousands of acre-feet of water remain stored and regularly replenished in the aquifer formed by the Raymond Groundwater Basin. Waters of the Arroyo Seco watershed, which stretches between La Cañada to the west and Santa Anita Canyon to the east, charge the aquifer below through percolation, as does the modest annual rainfall. In its north-south axis, the Arroyo Seco watershed runs from the base of the San Gabriel Mountains to the Raymond Fault. It is the earthquake fault that, under the surface of the earth, forms the Raymond Basin's southern perimeter, separating it from the Main San Gabriel Basin in a seven-mile run through the border of Pasadena and South Pasadena, and on through San Marino and Arcadia.

A cousin of the huge San Andreas Fault, the Raymond Fault is responsible for the San Rafael Hills in San Marino and Pasadena, where our story takes place. It runs directly under the campus of the Huntington Library, Art Museum, and Botanical Gardens. The Huntington mansion, built in 1910, is elegantly perched on the hill formed by the fault's tectonic energy enacted over time.

Moving west, the Raymond Fault forms the hills in the nearby neighborhoods of Highland Park, Dodger Stadium, and on through Griffith Park and Silver Lake. As it approaches the Pacific Ocean, the fault makes the Santa Monica Mountains and, once it goes under the Pacific Ocean, the northern Channel Islands. The Raymond Fault caused a 4.9 earthquake ten miles below Pasadena in December 1988.

The Raymond Fault makes a subterranean shelf or wall called the Raymond Dike, behind which the wet alluvial soils, sands, and rock in the aquifer back up. It is the fault that is responsible for the ancient ponds and swamps that once dotted the landscape just to the north of where it gouged the earth so far below the surface.

Some eight to ten thousand years ago, indigenous people settled here because of all this water. Thanks to the geology and seismic features of the aquifer and its associated fault, springs and seeps marked the terrain. The Tongva people probably arrived in the region sometime around three to four thousand years ago, coming from the east. The Tongva lived in small settlements necklaced atop the aquifer on an east-west axis, much like the shape that Huntington Drive takes today.

Franciscan missionaries moved the San Gabriel Mission here in 1776 for the fresh water, and because they knew where to find the indigenous people. The original mission had been built fifteen miles away, near present-day Whittier, in 1771, the fourth in a chain of missions that would eventually number twenty-one. Following a destructive flash flood, the Franciscans re-built their mission in the San Gabriel Valley to the north and west. The agriculturalists, vintners, and ranchers who came later all put down wells—lots of wells—and then roots. By the middle of the nineteenth century, the San Gabriel Valley boasted some of the most productive agricultural land in all of California.

Southern California has a Mediterranean climate. Mediterranean climates, which are not quite deserts, receive their rain in the winters, mostly from December through March. Summers are generally dry. Weather is temperate. With enough water, anything and everything grows.

Chapter 5

IF THE WELL EVER HAD a cap or cover, it was no longer in place on the afternoon of April 8, 1949.[1] As Alice, Jeanette, and Hamilton converged on the scene, more adults came to see what was the matter. They tried to figure out how deep the well went down. Kathy screamed and cried from far below.

Her uncle Hamilton, who was on crutches with an injured knee, frantically tried to lower a crutch into the well's mouth. But Kathy was too far below, the mouth of the well too narrow.

A neighbor, Robert Tibor, brought over a roll of telephone or electrical cord and the adults unspooled it into the well. Kathy could not hold onto it, and it was clear that she had fallen a long way down a very deep hole. As her mother remembered, "We realized that it was deeper and deeper and deeper all the time."[2]

At the San Marino police station, Desk Officer Earl Bliss logged a frantic call on a small card. The station—still there—is a half mile from the well, at the southeast corner of Huntington Drive and San Marino Avenue. A half dozen San Marino police officers, nearly a third of the force, raced to the well site. Alice, Jeanette, and Hamilton, along with their neighbor Robert Tibor, called to Kathy far below. She answered them faintly, crying and screaming.

"Can you hear me, Kathy?"

"Yes," she answered.

"Are you standing up, Kathy?"

"Yes."

"Are you lying down, Kathy?"

"Yes."

The situation grew frantic. The police officers radioed the fire department. Bring ropes. Five or six firemen soon clustered by the well with everyone else—family, neighbors, the police, the other children. No one knew what to do.

About an hour after Kathy fell in, the first newspaperman arrived. *Los Angeles Times* reporter Bill Johnston covered the San Gabriel Valley, and someone had told him to go to the scene.[3]

"I saw a few cars parked and housewives standing in front of their homes, aprons on, looking in the direction of the field," he remembered. Neighbors continued to bring things over to drop down the well. Nothing was long enough to reach Kathy, who was still crying down below. "I have never heard a more heartbreaking sound," Johnston wrote.[4]

Friends of the Fiscuses, the Metz family, arrived. They were supposed to have dinner with the Fiscus and Lyon families that night. Thinking that ten-year-old Nancy Metz, who was tiny, might fit into the well and could go down for Kathy, Barbara Fiscus measured her waist. Gus Lyon remembers that a firefighter did the same to him, which he found terrifying.[5]

Don Metz was an engineer for the Byron Jackson Pump Company. He found a mirror and, as the sun continued to wane, used it to try to throw light down the well. He began to cry. David Fiscus arrived. Alice had called him at his office nearby, where he was a manager for a local water company. His job included, or had until very recently, management of the old wells in the very field that was now the scene of so much chaos and worry.[6] In a horribly ironic twist, Dave Fiscus had just returned home, perhaps that very afternoon, from testifying in Sacramento to the California legislature on the dangers posed by abandoned wells that, unless they were properly capped or sealed, might bring contaminants into groundwater. He urged state officials to better regulate and police old wells. Any that had ceased functioning needed to be permanently closed off or destroyed.[7]

Johnston watched as Dave Fiscus began to pace in an unbearable choreography of worry. He "kept moving toward and away from the hole, standing up, sitting down, lying flat with his head in the hole, standing up, walking away, rubbing his hands and his head, his face suddenly contorting in an effort to keep his emotion from overflowing."[8]

Paul Barton, the San Marino city engineer, received a call from the plumbing inspector telling him that the little Fiscus girl had fallen into a storm drain. Barton asked him about the location and, upon hearing that it was in the field out back of the Fiscus home, said, "There's no storm drain there." He rushed over.

When Barton arrived, Dave Fiscus met him. "Paul, isn't there anything you can do?" he asked. Barton got on the phone and began calling contractors he knew, contractors who had machinery able to dig deep into the earth. He got hold of one with the firm Atwood and Purcell. They had a big clamshell digger out in the field in Los Angeles, and the contractor said he would rush it right over. The digger came north up the Arroyo Seco Parkway—normally not allowed for heavy equipment—accompanied by a motorcycle escort hastily ordered by the Pasadena chief of police.

First responders called the Pasadena Fire Department, a bigger outfit with a brand-new, all-purpose rescue vehicle. Pasadena fire-fighter Lloyd Van Buskirk, who drove the new rig over, thought at first that there had been a drowning, because people had clustered in a field near the Rubio Wash. Or maybe someone had been buried by dirt in an accident. It was hard to know what was going on. Van Buskirk, who was the rescue squad operator for the fire department, jumped out of his big truck. "What do you have here?" he asked the crowd.

"Well, there's a child down this hole," someone said.

The terrible truth dawned on Van Buskirk. "We looked down there, and we could hear, we could hear that little baby down there crying. And I'll never forget it. It's just—it's haunted me all my life.

First responders arrive at the scene early in the evening of April 8.

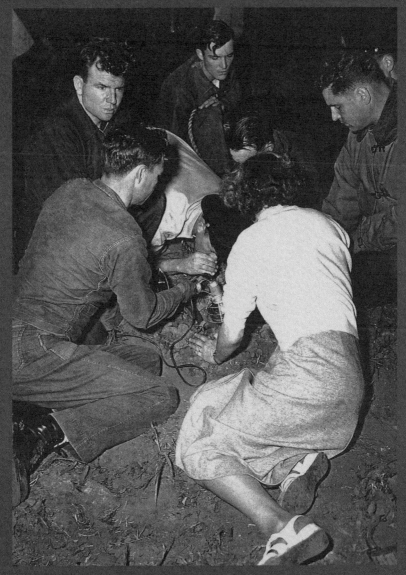

Kathy's aunt, Jeanette Lyon, at the mouth of the Johnson Well.

And so, they had a rope down in the hole. And they'd lowered it down the pipe. And we lowered a light. We had all kinds of auxiliary lights and so forth. And we lowered a light and realized that even down at the end of it, it disappeared. There was an elbow in that pipe."[9]

It looked as though Kathy had slipped below the bend way, way down.

Lloyd Van Buskirk and the other firefighters tied their rope to the one that had already been lowered down the well, tying a bowline loop in it to form a kind of lasso. The plan was to see if Kathy, still crying, could get the loop over her head and under her arms below her shoulders. Once the rope had been lowered down, those up top asked Kathy if she had hold of it. Though she was crying, she answered, "Yes." The firefighters asked her to pull on the rope, and they felt a gentle tug. They told her she should make sure to raise her arms so that the rope could go round her waist.

The rescuers now faced an awful dilemma: Should they pull on the rope or not? If they did, how hard should they pull? Would Kathy be able to get the rope around herself to sit below her shoulders, under her arms? In their frantic attempt to save her life, would they end up strangling her? Down the well, the rope had grown taut. Maybe she had it around her in the right way, maybe not. Maybe the rope had just snagged on a jagged part of the rusty well casing.[10]

The firefighters turned to David and Alice Fiscus. "We asked the parents to make a decision about what they wanted us to do," said Van Buskirk, "to pull tighter or what. And God, it was awful. Because they had no way of knowing—nor did we—what the situation was."[11]

Jeanette Lyon at the scene.

The firefighters made an effort. Then they stopped. It was too dangerous. David Fiscus and Dr. Robert McCulloch, a junior associate of the Fiscus family physician who had rushed to the scene, asked them to stop.

Kathy's cries, McCulloch said later, sounded like "a child shut in a dark closet. There wasn't pain in it, just bewilderment."[12] That seems wrong, even disingenuous, given firefighter Van Buskirk's memory. An ambulance or two showed up, ready to whisk Kathy off to St. Luke's Hospital, to the north against the San Gabriel

Fiscus family physician Robert McCulloch and a portable oxygen pump.

Mountains. At some point, Dr. McCulloch went to St. Luke's to wait.

Over by the Santa Anita Racetrack, just a few miles east on Huntington Drive, a motorcycle policeman told Tommy Francis that a little girl had fallen into a well. Twenty-six years old, Francis was a car guy who would later have an illustrious career in Mexican road racing. He had tools, welding equipment, and the like with him, and he drove to the site. He got there right around sunset, which would have been just before 6:30 p.m. He would stay there for the next fifty-eight hours.[13]

Chapter 6

THE HISTORY OF WATER and wells, and of aquifers and commerce, scaffolds the infrastructure of the Kathy Fiscus story like the scenery on the stage of a play. But what of the histories of the people whose lives were irrevocably changed in the spring of 1949 atop all that water? What about the human infrastructures of lineage: immigration and migration, grandparents, parents, and children?

How far back to start? One of the Fiscus ancestral paths takes us to upstate New York. This is where Henry Edwards Huntington's life began as well, the man who would one day own the Johnson Well and the field around it. Dead since 1927, Henry Huntington would have been a year shy of a hundred years old when the events of April 1949 unfolded within sight of his mansion in San Marino, California. Such are the patterns ever present in American history. One strand leads to another, and then another, and those strands, seemingly inevitably, often twist together. Families that once lived near one another did so again, across a continent and a century. In this case, however, the paths diverged: one went toward great wealth and power, and the other headed toward a much more commonplace existence.

Compared with the Huntington lineage, the Fiscus family tree looks positively modest. The Fiscus line is a far more typical family

in details of immigration and westering in America in the nineteenth and twentieth centuries.

At around the time of Henry Huntington's 1850 birth, James
Loveland, Kathy Fiscus's great-grandfather, was born in Ireland. He
came over the water, as countless Irish men, women, and children
did in the middle of the century, chased out by the awful hunger of
the Great Famine. In the depths of the horrible famine, one third
of the people of Ireland died. Another third stayed put. And a third
left. James Loveland ended up in Osceola, New York, a tiny ham-
let a scant one hundred miles from Henry Huntington's village of
Oneonta. They probably never saw one another, almost certainly
never met. One hundred miles was a long way in the nineteenth
century.

By the end of that terrible war, James Loveland owned his own
farm, worth about $1,500, and he could add to that sum about $300
of personal wealth. He was not exactly rich but not desperate, either, especially when we imagine the troubles he had surely known
back home in Ireland. Katarina Dixon (or Dickson), called Kitty,
was his wife. Born in Canada around 1847, Kitty was the daughter
of an Irish émigré father and a mother who may have been born
in England or possibly—the record is spotty—in Cuba (though the
name Katarina is of Czech origin). Around the time of the Civil
War, Kitty was in the United States, also in upstate New York. Soon
thereafter, she married James Loveland. Illiterate for the first half
of her life, Kitty learned to read and write sometime in the 1870s. By
1900, Kitty and James no longer lived together, although she was
still in Osceola. James may have been dead by then, but the census
did not refer to Kitty as a widow. Our view into the past is always
murky, opaque.

Kitty Dixon Loveland had eleven children. Or ten. The 1900 census counts eleven. The 1910 census counts ten. In 1900, eight or nine of those however-many children were still living. Six of them lived with their mother. Three of Kitty's children brought regular income into the household. Josephine was a schoolteacher, Isabelle was a stenographer, and Howard worked with mules.[1] By 1910, Kitty's household included four of her adult children, as well as her son-in-law James Homer Fiscus, and her three-year-old grandson David Fiscus.[2] She later moved with the Fiscus family to Camden Town (now Camden), New York, where she was no longer listed as the head of the household but seemed to still be married.[3]

James Homer Fiscus, was born in Pennsylvania in the fall of 1877.[4] By the turn of the century, he was a lodger in Utica, New York, where he worked as a druggist.[5] He married Kitty's daughter Elizabeth in 1906 or 1907, when she was about twenty-five and he about five years older.[6]

Kitty and some of Elizabeth's siblings moved in with them for a time. Homer eventually ran his own pharmacy.[7] In 1918, when he was forty, he registered for the draft not long after the United States entered the First World War.

By 1920, Elizabeth and Homer had two children, David and Elizabeth, and lived in Camden Town, where Homer continued to work as a pharmacist.[8] By the earliest years of the Great Depression, the Fiscus family had moved all the way across the nation to San Diego. That had to have been a big change in lives that had formerly been bounded by small and rural eastern hamlets. In San Diego County, they lived on Sweetwater Dam Road in a house they rented for thirty dollars a month. Homer Fiscus changed careers; in California, he worked as an overseer of the Sweetwater Reservoir owned by the Sweetwater Water Company.[9] We do not know when he died. Elizabeth died in 1957.[10]

That Fiscus line, traveling from upstate New York to California, brings us to David Fiscus, husband of Alice and father to Barbara and Kathy. David H. Fiscus was born in upstate New York, probably Utica, the day after Christmas in 1907. He was still living there as a teenager in 1920.[11] By the time he turned twenty-two, David had finished his schooling and was working as a civil engineer in San Diego County, near or probably at the Sweetwater Reservoir. Though his employer was not listed on the 1930 Census, he likely worked for the local public utility, where his father oversaw the irrigation reservoir and his sister Elizabeth was a stenographer.[12]

By 1935, through a series of acquisitions and mergers, the Sweetwater Water Company had become part of the California Water & Telephone Company (CW&T).[13] David Fiscus went to work for that new outfit just about the time the company began to buy up land and irrigation rights, properties, and projects across Southern California. California Water & Telephone ran a San Gabriel Valley Division, a Monterey Peninsula Division, and a San Diego Bay Division. All told, it bought up several dozen water and telephone companies by the middle of the century. A corporate headquarters in San Francisco sat atop all of it.

Alice Fiscus's grandfather, Chester Kinmore, was born in Wisconsin in 1855.[14] Again, we encounter water. As a young man, Chester secured homesteading title to 160 acres of land in Lac Qui Parle (French for "lake that speaks") County in western Minnesota.[15] That must not have worked out, because within five years, Chester had moved to Hennepin County and become a painter in Minneapolis.[16] In 1905, the Minnesota State Census listed his occupation as real estate.[17] He died in Hennepin County on July 10, 1908.[18] Chester Kinmore and his wife Dora had a son, Elmer, born on April 24, 1886, in a part of Dakota Territory that later became South Dakota.[19]

In 1905, at age nineteen, Elmer was living on his own in Hennepin, Minnesota.[20] There he met Ida Riebe, whose father Charles was a German immigrant. They married sometime not long after. By the time of the First World War, they were living in Chula Vista, California, ten miles south of San Diego and about the same distance from the Mexican border. Elmer, who went by "Win" because of his middle name, Winshie, worked as a supervisor for the Hercules Powder Company. Hercules came into being in the years just before the First World War, when the federal government trust-busted the DuPont explosives monopoly. On tidelands next to the ocean, the men working at Hercules extracted potash and acetone from kelp, which they then turned into explosives and munitions for use by the Allies in the First World War.[21] Kelp drawn from the Pacific Ocean off the coast of California helped win the war six thousand miles away.

Win Kinmore appears to have been a little restless. By 1920, the Kinmore family had moved to Lowell, Arizona, in the mining district near Bisbee. There Win worked as a repairman in a battery shop, receiving help from his father-in-law Charles Riebe, who was then living with the family.[22] They all soon returned to Chula Vista, where they raised their children, Alice, Jeanette, and Charles. Win ran an electrical appliance store.[23] Alice M. Kinmore was born on November 6, 1917, in San Diego County.[24]

The Kinmores raised Alice, Jeanette, and their kid brother, Charles, in this home when the family returned from their brief sojourn to Arizona. Charles, a high school athlete and fine student, died at sixteen in early 1932 when his appendix burst.

Alice met and married David Fiscus.[25] Their daughter, Barbara Jean, was born in 1940. Not long after, the little family moved to San Marino, where David had been transferred by his employer, the California Water & Telephone Company. He had been promoted to district manager.[26]

San Marino was not Chula Vista or San Diego, and it did not want to be. The *San Marino Tribune* crowed that the town was the "Finest Exclusively Residential City in the Entire West." David's region of responsibility covered a large portion of the San Gabriel Valley. On August 21, 1945, only weeks before the end of World War II, Alice gave birth to another little girl. David and Alice named their baby Kathryn Anne Fiscus.

When they first moved to San Marino, the Fiscus family lived in a home on Westhaven Road. But by 1946, when Kathy was an infant and Barbara was about six, they lived nearby in a small white house at 2590 Robles Avenue. Dave Fiscus's office, the regional headquarters of California Water & Telephone, was just to the west at 2130 Huntington Drive. Out back of the house was the field where we began this story. Close by stood an ancient adobe, the old Miguel Blanco Adobe near Rubio Wash, which carried water down from the mountains.

Alice Fiscus could work in the kitchen of the house on Robles and look out the window to that vacant field where the neighborhood children and Jeepers liked to play.

Given his district manager responsibilities, Dave Fiscus was in charge of that field with its old wells scattered here and there, some working, some not. Among them was the Johnson Well.[27]

Dave and Alice Fiscus, sitting on their porch in fearful vigil.
Alice Fiscus sat in the family Studebaker while the rescue attempt dragged on.

Chapter 7

BACK AT THE RESCUE SITE, no one was in charge. Or more accurately, there were too many people in charge. Firemen from Pasadena and San Marino. Their police counterparts. Los Angeles County Sheriff Eugene Biscailuz showed up. There was some technical know-how among them: Paul Barton had experience with big equipment, as did Don Metz, the Fiscus family friend and engineer. David Fiscus knew water, and he knew the well and the site. But he was distraught, chain-smoking and moving around the well in a daze. Alice Fiscus sat in the family Studebaker about a hundred yards away, "her lips compressed with the suffering that only a mother knows." Family and friends kept vigil with her. Word went out to her parents.

Once the rope plan had been rejected for fear of injuring Kathy, would-be rescuers put forth several ideas as to how they might proceed. Would someone go down the well and try to grab Kathy? Would a rescue shaft be sunk parallel to the Johnson Well so rescuers could break into her rusty trap from the side, and pull her out and up to safety?

The challenges were many, the confusion rampant. It was near dark. The well was clearly very deep, and there was concern that the metal casing lining the hole had a bend in it. If so, would their efforts cause Kathy to drop below that elbow—if she hadn't already—making rescue all the more difficult? Urgency reigned. Skinny Tommy Francis said he wanted to go down the hole to get Kathy.

Denied that chance, Tommy said he told the others to get a well digger on the scene as quickly as possible. No sooner had he said

Dave Fiscus is consoled at the scene by Pasadena's fire chief.

it than a clamshell digger, the kind with the giant clawed scoops, rolled up. "Jesus, here I look out in the street and here's a great big rig coming . . . with a clamshell on it," Francis remembered. It was the one that Paul Barton had requested, the one that had raced north on the freeway with a police escort. The digger quickly began to tear into the earth near the old well. The idea was to excavate a pit, lower men down it, and have them cut into Kathy's well and grab her.

Word traveled fast, as one would expect. A little girl trapped in a well. Crowds began to arrive, although city workers in San Marino attempted to barricade street access.[2] The Red Cross showed up, offering the rescue workers coffee and milk, along with doughnuts, pie, sandwiches, and cigarettes. A neighbor, Mrs. Burdette Cogswell, staffed the Red Cross support operation (called the San Marino Canteen Corps). "Funny how simple your tastes get at a time like this," a rescue worker said. "Bologna is just like chicken à la king."[3]

With the support of the firefighters on scene, Red Cross workers also helped operate an air pump. A hose attached to the pump was dropped into the well to try to ventilate it.[4] Years later, Tommy Francis insisted that he could see Kathy down in the well—perhaps by bouncing light off a mirror down the shaft—and that the vibrations and sheer weight of the clamshell digger caused her to slip further down.

Over in the brown sedan, Alice Fiscus sat in silence. At some point that evening, her parents arrived to join her. As more and more press showed up—newspaper reporters, radio broadcasters— friends and neighbors tried to shield Alice from prying cameras or reporters. One man kicked a photographer in the stomach. The *Los*

One of the clamshell diggers that excavated the big pit.

Angeles Times reporter, Bill Johnston, suggested to Alice that "the story had become much bigger than any of us."[5]

Not long after sunset, Kathy stopped crying.[6] At the scene, Fiscus family physician Dr. Paul Hanson said he believed Kathy to be safe, though likely unconscious. Still and motion picture cameras, some used for oil well work, were lowered into the shaft, but they either did not work or did not reveal anything; it was too dark at that point, and the cameras either malfunctioned or the lenses fogged over.

Kathy Fiscus

Right alongside the well Kathy had fallen into, the big clam-shell digger continued to chew the earth, pulling out soil, sand, and boulders. The going was tough: the damp, alluvial soil would fall in from the sides after each grab. Progress was slow: ten feet, then twenty, then thirty. Workers shuttled equipment to and fro, ran electricity lines, carried away dirt.

A camera is lowered down the mouth of the well. It did not work.

Big lights were brought in by an industrial supply firm in Pasadena. Within a day, these would be joined by motion picture Klieg lights sent over by Twentieth Century Fox. Before it was all over, as many as fifty floodlights turned night to day at the site.

Reporters kept coming. Porta-potties. Onlookers. Neighbors. Kids on bikes. Cars. A line of parked cars stretched a mile or more in multiple directions from the site. Volunteers came, thinking they might help somehow. Some in the assembled crowd wept, some prayed, some did both.

Clamshell diggers.

As the crowd of onlookers grew through the weekend,
ropes kept people back from the rescue scene.

Around 8:00 p.m., Leigh Wiener showed up. Just nineteen
years old, Wiener was a budding photographer with a gopher's job
at the *Los Angeles Times*, trying to get his foot in the door at the
paper. He later described the scene as "a carnival in full swing." He
saw vendors peddling food to a crowd he thought already had two
thousand onlookers. Some authorities said that the workers would
not get to Kathy for several days. Others suggested it was only a
matter of hours.

Wiener wandered around the site and walked over toward the
Fiscus home. On the front steps sat Gus, Stanley, and Barbara. The
little terrier was sitting on Barbara's lap. Wiener introduced himself and asked if he could take their picture. "Without a trace of
self-consciousness and almost in unison, they said, 'Sure.'"

Little Gus asked Wiener if he could have the burned-out

flashbulbs from the camera. Wiener gave them to him. Gus said he wanted to show Wiener the swing that he and Kathy played on. The kids led him to the swing in the backyard. "Near it were other tools of play, a wheeled hobby horse and an old tire casing," Wiener said. "The scene was simple. No confusion."

Another expert engineer showed up, sometime around midnight on Friday. Raymond Hill was not much liked by those who worked for him, but he was efficient and knowledgeable.[7]

With the tacit approval of the police and fire authorities, Hill took over the rescue operation, with Don Metz playing a key role alongside him. Important to the effort, too, was the very successful sewer contractor Mark Nottingham. Not everyone was pleased with Hill being in charge, giving orders. Tommy Francis remembered that rescue worker Whitey Blickensderfer turned to him and said that the "son of a bitch don't know nothing about dirt. He don't know a goddamn thing about dirt. What's he here for?"[8]

The rescue scene from the air. The Fiscus home is beneath the trees at top right. Note the line of cars parked along Winston Avenue.

Chapter 8

TWO RESCUE OPERATIONS were in motion, each dangerous. One involved digging the big shaft alongside and just south of the well. Once the parallel pit had gone down far enough—it would have to go below where Kathy was trapped—the plan was to dig a tunnel to the old Johnson Well casing, cut it open, and drag Kathy out. Another plan (or more accurately, a notion) focused on trying to get someone down the well to pull Kathy up and out the way she had gone in, much as Tommy Francis wanted to do when he first showed up at the site. Each approach was marked by increasingly frantic behavior, not least because Kathy's cries had clearly ceased. Alice Fiscus said later that she and her husband simply hoped that their presence and voices atop the earth had soothed their daughter and that she had gone to sleep, much as a frightened child in a darkened room eventually drops off.

The rescuers and other individuals who showed up either brought or tried to round up skinny men and boys to lower down into the well, so they might grab Kathy and bring her up. Anyone attempting this would have to be lowered head first into the well by his or her feet. Jockeys were hustled over from nearby Santa Anita Racetrack and from Hollywood Park in Inglewood, about twenty-five miles away. A call went out to Hollywood casting agents and the Screen Actors Guild for people with dwarfism or other "little people" characteristics; someone had an idea to try to find "Munchkin" actors from *The Wizard of Oz*.

That plea for a diminutive person was answered by none other than Johnny Roventini, the less-than-four-foot-tall Philip Morris "callboy" who—branded as the "living trademark" that he most assuredly was—appeared at the scene in his full bellhop costume.

It could not get any stranger. But it did. A circus performer, the "thin man" from Clyde Beatty's Circus, showed up and volunteered to go down. Some reports say that three circus thin men showed up to try to help. Several people arrived to volunteer their own children as rescuers who could be lowered down into the well. None were small enough, or none wanted to get dropped into the narrow darkness of the old well.

At the scene, David Fiscus was reluctant to have anyone else go into the well; he vetoed any scheme to send someone down there. According to Tommy Francis, Dave Fiscus erupted at one point when ideas about putting someone down the Johnson Well were being discussed. "I'll have the goddamn hole covered up right now, if that man goes down that hole," Francis remembered Fiscus saying. "I'll have it covered up. We'll call it her grave."[1]

Friends and neighbors consoled Dave and Alice Fiscus as they, along with Alice's family, moved back and forth between the scene, their car, and their house. The press mostly left them alone, although some reporters attempted to interview one or the other of them. At the house, loved ones tried to get them to rest, to lie down. Dr. Hanson provided sedatives. The pastor of the brand new Congregational Church nearby on Huntington Drive arrived. The Reverend Bertrand Crist had baptized Kathy only five months earlier, one of the thirteen children baptized at the church in 1948. As

Kathy Fiscus

Johnny Roventini at the scene. Rescuers planned to lower him down the Johnson Well, but Dave Fiscus would not allow it.

Alice's parents waited and worried, they must have been thinking of an earlier tragedy that had hit their family: the loss of their only son, Charles, struck down years earlier by a burst appendix at age sixteen. His sister Alice had found him.[2]

As Friday night went on, the parallel pit became the paramount rescue operation. Even though any expectation of lowering someone down the impossibly narrow opening fell by the wayside, authorities were besieged with telephone, telegram, and face-to-face suggestions from near and far, each offering generally untenable ideas as to how to save the little girl. Newspaper reports claim that the suggestions numbered in the thousands. A woman arrived with her five-year-old daughter in tow. Another came with her thin son, offering to send him down. A local physician proposed that a vacuum could be created in the well so that Kathy could be sucked up to safety. Equipment to accomplish this was actually secured, but the plan did not go anywhere. Someone else suggested that water could be slowly poured into the well—someone else proposed sand—and Kathy would magically rise to the surface.

That these far-fetched ideas were even suggested, much less considered, along with the idea of Hollywood or circus performers suspended upside down and lowered into the narrow darkness, is an indication of the feverish nature of the rescue effort and its astounding challenges. The scene itself had become a circus, albeit one marked by desperation, heroism, and frenetic activity.

A thermometer lowered into the well came back up with a ninety-degree reading. Near midnight, authorities lowered a five-inch

Opposite: Barbara Fiscus and cousin Stanley Lyon
await news at a neighbor's home.

rubber ball, weighted with sand, into the well, attached to an unspooling tape measure. When it stopped falling, presumably because it had bumped into the trapped little girl, they pulled it back up again. It came back dry after traveling down nearly ninety feet.

Kathy Fiscus had fallen nine stories down.

The assembled crowd at night. People sang, held hands, and prayed.

Chapter 9

DIGGING CONTINUED throughout the early hours of Saturday morning, bright lights cascading across what had so recently been an empty, weeded field near the new elementary school. Emergency vehicles, tools, and miscellaneous equipment lay strewn around the area. Onlookers spent the night on the site, sleeping on blankets on nearby lawns, propped up in folding chairs, sipping thermos coffee. Hastily erected fences and ropes kept the crowds back, away from the well itself, in concentric boundaries. First came the chaotic rescue scene itself, and then the press at about fifty feet; farthest back was the swelling crowd. As many as 250 law enforcement personnel were present: highway patrolmen, police officers from several towns, the LAPD, and county sheriffs. One newspaper report, showing a map of the site, said the location was inhabited by "an army of hard-rock miners, engineers, midgets, jockeys, police, firemen, and spectators."[1]

Vendors worked the scene, selling hot dogs, ice cream, and even liquor.[2] The crowd seems to have been largely quiet, even dazed. People sat, stood, milled around, climbed trees, cried, prayed, and whispered. A prayer group of thirty people arrived and asked to be admitted to the site to offer continual prayer. Kathy's sister, Barbara, eventually went to stay with the Metz family, where they watched the rescue operation on television. But for a time, she and her cousins Gus and Stanley, along with Jeepers, awaited news along with everyone else. Police authorities would later say that they received calls from every state in the nation inquiring about the progress of the rescue effort.

A couple of hours before daybreak, the big pit dug beside the well had gone approximately sixty-five feet into the earth. Workers had started to dig a tunnel connecting it to the well that held Kathy, even though she was far below that point. The tunneling aspect of the work was by far the most dangerous. At least the pit

Both rescue excavations: the big pit and the narrow rescue shaft lined with casing. *Opposite*: A close-up view of the pit dug alongside the old well.

Another view of the big rescue pit that was abandoned in favor of the narrower hole lined with casing.

had a hole at the top; any tunnel would be a fragile horizontal shaft atop which pressed countless tons of earth and sand.

Rescuers raised concerns that the big hole would collapse in on itself. Maybe it was too big—it looked like a smaller version of an open-mine copper pit, after all—and the soil was sandy and moist. Would it hold? Would it increasingly become a danger to the workers who labored within it? Though it went far down, it would do no good unless it could first be dug past the ninety-foot depth where Kathy was wedged.

By 7:00 or 7:30 on Saturday morning—around seventeen hours after Kathy had tumbled into the well—the pit had gone down about seventy-seven feet. As the sun rose, Albert Linell, a former salvage diver in the US Navy, tunneled across to the old well, wearing a safety harness to connect him to the top of the adjacent hole. The call went out for everyone up top to hush. With all machinery turned off and the huge crowd gone completely silent, Linell placed his head and a microphone close to the rusted metal, somewhere not too far above where they thought Kathy lay trapped, trying to hear any sound from within. The microphone lowered into the pit picked up Linell's voice, suspended in the hole. "Can't hear a thing," he said, his words echoing out to the crowd. "I can't hear a thing."

The digging continued. By 8:30 a.m., the pit was between eighty and eighty-five feet deep. They were so close. Within the hour, the workers had gone far enough to cut a window in the wall of the old well casing, just above the little girl. It took about two hours to do it. Just before noon, workers believed they had spotted Kathy's dress and part of her arm down below, at about the ninety-foot level.

Then work on the pit stopped. Loose dirt and stones had started to fall on the suspended rescuers from the sides of the pit as they worked, and rescue leaders were afraid it would cave in. Exhaustion, anxiety, uncertainty, and confusion ran parallel to engineering skill and earth-moving experience at the site. Less accomplished (or, at least, less educated) men at the scene—miners, cesspool diggers, former Navy Seabees—argued with the men with engineering degrees. It would be better, they insisted, to dig a narrower hole next to the well, one that would not fall in. "Let us do it," they said. "We know how to dig, and a well-digging auger can help us. Get these big clamshells out of here. The pit is unstable; the weight of the machinery will shake the little girl further down the well." Back off, they insisted. The scene became heated, tense, and argumentative.

These men carried the day. Of course, everyone wondered if it would be too late. By Saturday evening, Kathy would have been down the well for twenty-four hours. The rescue effort now concentrated on the second of two excavations—this one more of a hole than a pit—which rescuers had begun to dig and drill even before the big pit was abandoned. Five feet from the Johnson Well, workers bored this second hole with well-digging equipment and hand-held digging and dirt-removal tools: buckets, spades, and picks.

The rescue scene.

About a hundred men—construction workers, former Navy Seabees, sewer and cesspool workers, and miners—worked on scene, though the corps of rescuers who spent time down either of the two holes was much smaller. In search of a foreman and a story, the press hit upon Homer Blickensderfer, whom the *Los Angeles Times* called "the titan of the entire project."[3] A high school dropout, the forty-three-year-old Blickensderfer, called "Whitey" because of his blond hair, had been a sailor in the Navy, a truck driver, a brick mason, an auto repairman, a tunneler on construction sites, and a carpenter. "That man of mine," his wife Frances told a reporter at the scene, "is good at sandhogging, mining, carpentering, mechanics, almost anything." Despite a painful hernia condition, Blickensderfer worked ceaselessly.[4]

Whitey Blickensderfer picked a group of men to do most of the work on the rescue tunnel in shifts. The press quickly dubbed them "sandhogs," diggers of construction projects underground or underwater. The men were lowered down into the hole standing on a crude elevator made from a thirty-gallon bucket, secured by cables to a crane. Down below, they worked in shifts.

These men, whose names, faces, and thumbnail biographies soon became known to onlookers and people literally across the world by way of news stories, included:

Bill Yancey, also known as "Bull." He had been an underwater demolitions man in the Navy Seabees during the war. Yancey's specialty was "exploding enemy mines that menaced American shipping." To reporters, he spoke of time spent in Okinawa, where he got a little girl out of a cave after she became trapped while trying to hide during a bombardment. Yancey had a San Gabriel sewer contracting business and was, as his partner's wife remembered him, "a big, strapping man."[5] When he first showed up at the well site to offer his help, county sheriffs and what were then called auxiliary sheriffs (civilian volunteers to the force, probably a holdover from the Second World War) had turned him away. Paul Barton knew Yancey, and he knew his skill set. Armed with a pickaxe handle to emphasize his point, Barton got Yancey admitted to the rescue operation.[6]

Yancey's business partner, Bartram "Herb" Herpel, was also sent down the shaft. Herpel had served with Yancey in the Seventy-First Construction Battalion in the Pacific during the war.[7] Given their experience during and after the war, it is likely that Yancey and Herpel insisted that the narrower hole be dug alongside the well. B. A. Gorham, Yancey's one-time employer, was a sewer contractor from nearby Temple City. He sent one of his well diggers to the scene—Mark Nottingham, the region's acknowledged expert in sewer and septic excavations. In the years following the Fiscus episode, Nottingham would build the world's largest sewer excavation company.

The rescue workers also included John Inaht, a former coal miner from Pennsylvania; Paul Neiford, also a former miner; Orpheus A. Kelly; and Clyde Harp. Up top, 270-pound Ned Larson (the papers called him a giant, in stark contrast to the little people also at the scene) worked non-stop lifting and discarding bucket after bucket of earth brought up the shaft. A woman watching the rescue effort on television called the KTLA switchboard at one point to say that she was (inexplicably) keeping track of the number of buckets that had come up full of dirt. When she called in, that tally had reached 191.[8]

By 3:00 p.m. on Saturday, the second rescue operation had dug

Whitey Blickensderfer. Called "Whitey" for his blond hair, Blickensderfer became the foreman of the rescue operation.

down about eighty feet. Rescuers believed that by midnight, they would reach the level where Kathy was trapped. But the work was slow and hard. The dirt had to be taken out of the hole, and the effort was slowed by big boulders that needed to be broken up and carried in pieces to the surface. Estimates for when they would reach Kathy moved past midnight to the early hours of Sunday morning.

To prevent the second rescue hole from crumbling, and to protect the rescuers who would go down after Kathy, the rescuers planned to line the hole with four sections of twenty-foot-long steel pipe. The first section was lowered into the hole once it had been dug and drilled down to near Kathy's level. It was about 8:00 p.m. on Saturday night. The first one went in the hole, then the next, the next, and the last. Each section was hoisted up by crane and guided into the hole, where it was lowered by cable (and gravity) and then pounded by a pile driver as far into the deepening hole as it could go. Section one was welded to section two, two to three, and three to four.

The rescue hole was completely lined with the casing sometime around 10:30 Saturday night. Inside the casing, where the men worked, the gap between the pipe and the bottom of the hole would allow the workers to dig their tunnel across the earth to Kathy. Inside the narrow metal tube, workers used a crushed galvanized bucket (which could fit into the narrow spaces down there) to carry dirt, sand, and rocks away. At one point, the entire casing was lifted up to provide the men with more room to work in the cavern.

Opposite: The casing that lined the second rescue excavation.

The feverish rescue scene is lit up by Klieg lights.

Kathy Fiscus

Gus and Stanley Lyon, Barbara Fiscus, and Jeepers.

Chapter 10

IN THE MEANTIME, the television men had shown up to join the other reporters and radio broadcasters. Two rival Los Angeles stations, KTTV and KTLA, arrived to film the rescue, each with trucks carrying generators that enabled live broadcasts from the chaotic scene.

This moment, which began as an experiment and a brainstorm, would turn out to be revolutionary. The Kathy Fiscus story would prove that television was a suitable medium for hard news, not just entertainment, moving it with one bold stroke beyond what it had been before, which was mostly an amusement in the family parlor: a little electric box where kids could watch puppet shows. Remote sports broadcasts had already taken place and were, in fact, somewhat common. But this was different. This was news—live news.

But it was not, in fact, the first remote TV news broadcast. Sixteen years earlier, the Long Beach earthquake slammed into the Southern California coastline. Though there were only a handful of television sets in Los Angeles at the time, viewers saw the destruction on station W6XAO's broadcast.[1] It may seem surprising that there was TV at all in the early years of the Great Depression; the invention we so confidently think of as a technological and cultural innovation of post-World War II has much earlier origins.

Another event in Los Angeles preceded the Kathy Fiscus saga.

On the morning of February 20, 1947, the O'Connor Electro-Plating Corporation, a chemical plant tucked into a mixed-use industrial and residential neighborhood on East Pico Boulevard near downtown Los Angeles, blew up. The blast killed seventeen people, and television reporters filmed the aftermath. KTLA arrived with studio cameras in a van and did remote filming of the devastation. The scene, which looked like a bombsite, went out over the airwaves as the first remote broadcast of breaking news in history. There were approximately 350 television sets in greater Los Angeles at the time.[2]

At the edge of the old Johnson Well in San Marino, KTLA and KTTV would end up broadcasting continuously for more than twenty-four hours. There were about 20,000 televisions in Los Angeles at this time, a huge jump from the number of people who would have been able to see the O'Connor explosion only two years before. Early televisions were expensive, hundreds of dollars, but the post-war economy in Los Angeles was strong.

At the time, television broadcast technology could only allow transmission for short distances. People who remember watching the rescue operation in locations beyond Los Angeles were watching newsreel, not live footage.[3] Locally, however, crowds congregated in front of appliance store windows all across greater Los Angeles. Store proprietors moved televisions to the front window displays, turned them on, and left them on. *Los Angeles Times* reporter Cecil Smith then knew "the potential of television when he saw crowds of people standing in front of storefronts, eyes glued to the television sets behind the glass."[4]

The Kathy Fiscus story ushered in the era of modern television journalism. "This is tragic," said one producer from KTLA, "but this is also television history." He was right on both counts. That producer was the visionary Klaus Landsberg. A television pioneer if ever there was one, Landsberg had learned his craft in his native Germany. Trained as an electrical engineer, he designed the first cathode-ray tube before turning twenty. After fleeing Germany, Landsberg worked on the 1939 World's Fair in New York before coming west to help establish a television station for Paramount Studios.

On Saturday morning, April 9, Landsberg called reporter Bill Welsh at home. Welsh, who had come to KTLA as a sports and general interest reporter in 1946, had heard about Kathy on the radio. As he remembered years later, Landsberg wanted Welsh to go out to San Marino to "see if we could televise from the scene."[5]

Welsh drove over from Burbank and met Landsberg and a small crew at the site. It took a while to get the equipment up and running, and it was all an experiment. "In those days," Welsh said, "nobody believed a television station could work continuously hour after hour."[6]

Television engineers thought the tubes and other equipment would give out, short circuit, or maybe even just melt. But the equipment did not break. At one point, Landsberg combined two transmitters by hand to supply more power to get the live feed out onto the airwaves. To make the broadcast work, the TV trucks had to have a "line of sight" to the top of Mount Wilson, where the KTLA transmitter sat. As luck would have it, they did. The station stopped airing all commercials, as well as any other broadcasting. For more than twenty seven hours, from late Saturday afternoon to deep into Sunday evening, live television was at the scene.

Television personality Stan Chambers joined Welsh at the site.

Television station **KTTV** broadcasting from the scene.
The cameras had a direct line of sight to a transmitter atop nearby Mount Wilson.

Kathy Fiscus

Little more than a cub reporter at the time and a station jack-of-all-trades, Chambers worked in sales and also hosted a show called *Meet Me in Hollywood,* where he interviewed people at the corner of Hollywood and Vine. Welsh and Chambers did the entire KTLA broadcast together.[7] The other station, KTTV, broadcast from the scene in snippets, alternating between filming the rescue, then stopping and starting up again with reporters in the shot.

It all began off-camera and inconspicuously. "What shall we say?" Welsh asked Landsberg. "Pretend it's a sporting event and give them the play-by-play," his boss responded, before turning to Chambers and advising him to "just watch Bill." Throughout the drama, Landsberg narrated human-interest stories from the site, passing them on to Welsh and Chambers through their earphones to be repeated word for word.[8]

The reporters also interviewed people. They interviewed the engineers in charge, one of whom explained the work on the narrow rescue hole: "We're going to hammer that casing about a hundred feet into the ground to a point below where Kathy is trapped. We have to get all of the dirt inside the casing, then go down to the bottom and cut a vertical tunnel across, shore it up with timbers and try to dig across the well pipe where we can get her."[9]

Over in nearby Temple City, a young man named Clyde Harp learned about the event while watching his brand-new nine-inch RCA television, the one with a fifty dollar convex bubble hooked onto the front to make the picture look bigger. The TV had cost Clyde $450. He saw what was happening at the site, and did not think the first pit excavation was a good idea. "Look at what they're doing," he said to his father-in-law.

Concerned that the clamshells and draglines were a waste of

KTTV and **KTLA** television cameras aim at the rescue attempt: watching, waiting, filming.

precious time as well as dangerous, since their weight and vibrations might jostle Kathy further down the well), Harp left his home
on Saturday without telling anyone and drove over to San Marino,
where he hopped the fence and made his way to the Johnson Well
site. He knew the area from the bread delivery route he drove. "You
aren't going about this right," he told the authorities when they
were still worrying over the big pit. "You need to just dig a hole."[10]

Twenty-five years old and already married with five kids, Clyde
Harp dug cesspools as a teenager. "I could throw a lot of dirt in an
hour," he said. He knew some of the men working at the well site,
and he pitched in at the second rescue hole. Asked why he had
come to help, Clyde responded that at home he had a six-week-old
baby girl, a two-year-old girl, a three-year-old boy, a five-year-old
girl, and a seven-year-old boy. His family only found out he was
there when they saw him on television back at home.

The work was both primitive and not. An upended bucket,
swung over and into the hole, allowed a harnessed rescuer to stand
on top of it and dig around the earth with a spade, dropping the
shaft ever lower through non-stop labor. A smaller bucket took out
the dirt. It sounds cumbersome, but somehow it worked. These
men knew what they were doing. They knew how to dig, they knew
how to get rid of dirt, and they knew how to work in tight spaces.

Welsh and Chambers had a microphone that picked up the
sounds of the ongoing effort, even of men singing as they chipped
away at the rock down below. They speculated about the rescue
operation. When they learned of things that were needed for the
rescue operation, they put out calls for special equipment: air-pow-
ered tools that would not create sparks or risk the possible shock or
electrocution caused by electrical tools. Supplies showed up.

Kathy Fiscus

The portable oxygen pump manned by Red Cross volunteers and first responders.

As workers came up out of the hole, they would be wrapped in blankets, given something hot to drink, and placed on cots. Chambers and Welsh interviewed them on-air, walking around with their microphones. The camera mostly focused on the two excavations underway, as well as the hand-cranked air pump that was constantly tended by a firefighter or other volunteer.[11] Radio reporters also broadcast the rescue effort nonstop from the scene, the most prominent among them Hank Weaver of KECA Radio.

While all this went on, more offers of help and bits of advice continued to pour in. Most were far-fetched ideas about how to bring Kathy up out of the well, or ways in which people could go down to get her. One man in Colorado volunteered to go down the Johnson Well for Kathy. Another man named J.W. Crays said he had gone to a local pipe supply store in his hometown of Pueblo and managed to squeeze into a pipe only twelve inches in diameter. "I then got into a 13¾-inch pipe and had lots of room."[12] A local woman from nearby San Gabriel sat with her two children at the scene and recalled an earlier, failed rescue attempt to get a spelunker out of a Kentucky cave. "I watched them dig for Lloyd [sic; it was Floyd] Collins in Kentucky, and I don't want to leave this now." Two sailors showed up at the well site and offered to help. One had been a miner in Colorado, and the other declared that he was "so darned small I can get into anything."[13]

Bill Welsh remembered the scene, the frantic activity. Workers, "real wild-eyed guys" went at it, he said, "taking terrible chances." Welsh almost fell into the pit once himself as he walked around it. "I was on the edge and somebody yelled at me and I turned away."[14]

Once the television reporters got rolling with their broadcasts, about 6 p.m. on Saturday night, the audiences fixated on Kathy's fate swelled to even larger sizes. Welsh later received letter after letter from people who had watched the broadcast. He recalled how these letters would often describe the sequence of events:

> When we first saw you on the air at eight o'clock in the evening we called the Joneses and they came over at about nine o'clock. And then at ten o'clock the Smiths heard about it and asked if they could come over, and they did. Midnight Suzie and Mary and I cooked up breakfast for the guys. And then at about two o'clock Joe and George went to sleep in the beds. . . .[15]

When the drilling or the casing hit boulders or tough rock formations, workers tried to dig around obstacles or smash them with their shovels and picks. With helmets on to provide light, and with lights shining down from the top, workers began to work on the lateral tunnel late Saturday night. They estimated they would reach Kathy by 3:00 a.m. on Sunday.

"I have not given up hope," Alice Fiscus told a reporter. "I have never felt that Kathy is anything but perfectly all right."

"All we can do," said Dave Fiscus, "is hope."[16]

While the rescue attempt continued nearby,
photographer Leigh Wiener shot this picture
of the swing at the Fiscus home.

Chapter 11

THE DIAMETER OF the steel-lined second shaft was twenty-four inches, and the hole in which it sat was slightly bigger. It made for a small space, but it was a full ten inches wider than the well that held Kathy Fiscus. When the well-digging equipment broke down at one point, workers reluctantly went back to the crumbling pit. But it was deemed too dangerous; rescuers had to wait until a new well digger showed up. In the pit below, the soil was sandy and wet and peppered with large boulders. The smaller hole was once again the focus of the main rescue effort.

Even though Raymond Hill was in charge of the rescue effort, Sheriff Eugene Biscailuz kept an eye on things, too. At one point, probably Saturday night, the sheriff approached Tommy Francis. Hill and Biscailuz wanted to take him off the job, or at least give him some rest. Francis had just been approached by a photographer who told him he would pay him $500 to take a picture in the pit below. Tommy took the camera from the photographer and then threw it as far as he could. Biscailuz and some others took Francis to the Red Cross tent under protest and gave him a ferocious rubdown, as if he were a lightweight boxer catching his breath between rounds.

Tommy Francis did not want to stop. "Look, you son of a bitch," he remembered telling Biscailuz, "I can outdo you or anybody here,

The rescue attempt continues with lengths of steel casing lowered one atop another as the hole deepened.

any goddamn day, for the next seventy-two hours. I'm in perfect health and I'll do anything. I'll run a fifty-yard or one-hundred-yard dash for you right goddamn now if you think I ain't physically well. And if you want to—if you want to test my reflexes, be my guest, goddamn it." Even thirty years later, his anger rose quickly to the surface when re-telling the encounter.

Biscailuz pulled a bullet from his belt bandolier and threw it at Francis. "I caught that son of a bitch one handed," Francis said. Needless to say, he went back to work.[1]

By the earliest hours of Palm Sunday, the second rescue shaft had been sunk deep enough to start tunneling across to the old

Kathy Fiscus

well as planned. But taking out all of the dirt was proving very difficult. It was sandy, and boulders were everywhere. Water, always on their mind, became a constant worry. It was wet down there.

Sometime after midnight, Herb Herpel came up after digging the rescue shaft down to just past ninety feet. It had to be dug just a bit below where the men thought Kathy was lodged, so that they could tunnel up to where they thought she was inside the Johnson Well. The rescuers were afraid that, with all the digging down below and the activity up top, there was a chance Kathy could slip further down the well. If they could get just below her, they could try to prevent that from happening and, they hoped, pull her to safety.

It turned out that the hard clay in the soil might be a good thing. It was hard to dig through, but Herpel and the others thought that, because of the clay, the little rescue cavern might not have to be shored up, saving valuable time. Maybe it would hold up on its own, without mineshaft timbers. Maybe the clay would keep water from the aquifer out of the tunnel.

Clyde Harp, who later described his younger self as weighing "150 pounds wringing wet," spent hours underground—digging, lining up the metal casing, getting dirt out of the hole fistfuls at a time. "Were you ever frightened?" he was asked. "Not in the hole," he said. "I had dug a lot of holes. It's just a hole. But that tunnel scared me. The whole thing could collapse and bury a man in an instant. It was like playing Russian roulette."[2]

A few hours before dawn on Palm Sunday, the protective casing of the shaft was lowered a few more feet. B.A. Gorham went down to investigate the tiny tunnel, along with Mark Nottingham. Rescuers figured that Kathy was not far away—inches at least, and a foot or two at most.

At dawn, tools were lowered so the workers could make their cut-through into the Johnson Well casing, as well as a microphoned public address system for the men to communicate their needs to those above ground. Herpel went down first; onlookers and the television audience soon picked up his swearing through the microphone. Then a scream. "I've hit water. It is coming in from all sides. Pull me up!" Then: "That's far enough. Let me check this water level . . . it's just oozing in . . . plenty of mud . . . but we'll just have to haul it out."[3]

Work stopped again soon thereafter. There was too much water. It had to be pumped out. The rescue effort had clearly gone right into the Raymond Basin water table, which made sense, of course—that was why the Johnson Well was there in the first place. There was an old pump house nearby, sitting atop another well not far from the ancient Michael White adobe. The pump house was called into service (most likely by David Fiscus, who was the boss of the landscape) to try to lower the water level below the rescue tunnel and maybe even within Kathy's well itself.

Whitey Blickensderfer went down again. Water was flowing into the rescue shaft at three gallons a minute. "Hot down there, really hot," Bill Yancey told television reporter Stan Chambers. "The big trouble was the rocks, big as your head, some of them, and hard to handle in that space."[4] According to Tommy Francis, water was "just seeping slowly in, from every direction, and we was bailing it out as fast as we could to keep working in there . . . we was hacking away like that and we'd shore around us as we went in. There was another man standing at the bottom of the hole just bailing, as fast as he could . . . at the end the water was seeping in so fast we didn't think we was going to make it."[5] But workers thought that the old

Johnson Well itself was dry, at least at the level at which Kathy was trapped.

The men left the cavern to give the pump a chance to work. It drew water out and drained it into a little reservoir nearby. It was slow going.[6] The flow into the shaft increased by mid-morning, putting the entire operation in jeopardy. They could not possibly dig a third hole. According to Francis, "It got so bad, I was laying on my belly, and when I lifted my head up my head hit the top of the hole that we was tunneling across, and the water was right here. So I had to back out, or they pulled me by the boots back out, cause the water was coming right up to my nose. Another ten minutes, I'd have drowned down there."[7]

Around nine in the morning on Palm Sunday, rescue worker Paul Neiford went down the shaft and determined that the water level had receded to a point where work could resume. Just after ten, workers cracked the old well open at a depth of ninety-four feet. This was not yet the window of rescue; it was only the beginning. Twigs, debris, and water spilled out. Kathy was presumed to be just a handful of inches above this point.

Above ground, it was a bright, sunny day. Thousands of people—some of whom had spent the night there, others who had just shown up in their hats, sundresses, and sunglasses—waited uneasily for news of Kathy's fate. As many as five thousand people were at the scene. As the day went on, the number would swell to as many as ten thousand. Other reports put the number even higher, at fifteen thousand or more, though that seems to be an exaggeration since San Marino barely had ten thousand residents at the time. Whatever the number, it's clear that a lot of people came to the fields and the fences, and many of them brought young children with them.

Hard or not, the clay would not hold in the tunnel. It started to give way because of the water pressing on it from behind. Workers lowered timbers down to prop it up. At lunchtime, three feet of wet sand fell into the tunnel, burying two of the rescuers in about eighteen inches of water. The workers, all trying to, in the words of *New York Times* reporter Gladwin Hill, "undo the cruel fluke of fate," were pulled free—exhausted and frightened but otherwise unhurt.[8]

On a break from digging, Clyde Harp drove all over the San Gabriel Valley looking for more pneumatic tools. It was hard to find a store open on Palm Sunday, but he finally ran across one in El Monte.

Down in the hole, the rescuers made requests via the pit's microphone. "Hello up there," one said. "Send the bucket down with the other set of tools in it. . . . Where is the chuck wrench for that machine? We are breaking a drill about every two inches. . . . Please send down the other bucket of tools."[9]

Clyde Harp remembered being enraged at one point when electrical tools came down to him while he stood in water. A bucket of heavy tools at the lip of the rescue shaft tipped over, cascading the tools down on top of Harp. He swore, upon which Mark Nottingham, the sewer contractor, shouted down at him, "Quit swearing down there. You're on television!"[10]

A small parachute harness came down the rescue shaft. The plan was to get it around Kathy, lift her up quickly, and then rush her off to St. Luke's Hospital, where Dr. Robert McCulloch and others waited.

Pneumatic drills gave way to pneumatic saws and grinders, so a twelve-by-eighteen-inch "window" could be cut into Kathy's well and she could be hauled out. Tommy Francis helped run drill bits

Kathy Fiscus

across the casing diameter below where they thought Kathy was lodged. This made a kind of metal skein designed to catch Kathy if she slipped further down the well as they reached in to get her. Workers believed she was not much more than a foot above the drill-bit lattice.

Again, work slowed. Cutting the rusty old Johnson Well casing broke the blades. Through the P.A. system, Whitey Blickensderfer announced that the workers were breaking one blade for every two to four inches of cutting. Orpheus Kelly and Blickensderfer spent more than two hours down the shaft, cutting away as best they could. By late afternoon, forty-eight hours after Kathy had fallen into the well, the crowd began to stir, sensing news.

Clyde Harp went down. Tommy Francis went with him. The window into Kathy's well was opened at last. Out poured, as Francis remembered, "bottles, tin cans, weeds, rags, newspapers, you name it." Francis said that Kathy herself was dry.[11] But there was water in the tunnel between her well and the rescue shaft—four feet of it, according to Blickensderfer—and the workers had to retreat again. The dripping sounded, Blickensderfer told reporters, "like bullets hitting the iron casing."[12]

The workers returned to cut a larger hole and discovered Kathy just below the window. "She was right there," Harp told me.[13]

But Kathy Fiscus was dead.

Chapter 12

THIRTY YEARS LATER, Tommy Francis remembered seeing tear stains on Kathy's face.

The crowd up top knew nothing for several hours. At around 5:30 p.m., Orpheus Kelly and Whitey Blickensderfer asked that their microphones be disconnected from the public address system up top. They huddled with Raymond Hill.

The air pump stopped at 6:00 p.m. At 6:03, Hill announced that Kathy had been sighted—he did not say whether she was alive or dead—at about the ninety-four-foot level in the Johnson Well. Workers lowered a "sling seat," something like a bosun's chair, down the rescue shaft by crane, then a folded-up stretcher. Both returned to the top empty. Asked if Kathy was alive, Hill offered only a terse, "I don't know." But he probably did.[1]

An ambulance backed up to the edge of the well at 6:35 p.m. Two rescue workers pulled gently on a rope that had been dropped down the hole. Firemen started up the air pump again. At 7:40 p.m., Orpheus Kelly was lifted out of the shaft, without Kathy. The crowd hushed and seemed to know then that things looked grim. At just after 8:00 p.m., Bill Yancey was swung over the shaft on the cabled bucket and lowered down.

Sometime around 8:00 p.m., Dr. McCulloch was summoned from St. Luke's Hospital. It had been decided that he would go down the shaft, though he didn't want to (he was probably claustrophobic). "It was a hell of a thing to do to a doctor," his senior partner remembered. "He was gutsy but scared to death anyway. It was very dramatic."[2]

At about 8:20 p.m., rescuers outfitted McCulloch in an odd getup: an aviator's cap, blue jeans, and the parachute harness hooked to a cable. His shirt was open, and he had on a pair of troopers' boots. "He looked like Clark Gable," Dr. Hanson recalled.[3] "He's a

Dr. Robert McCulloch, harnessed in a parachute vest, about to be lowered down the rescue casing.

Fiscus family physician **Paul Hanson** makes his announcement Sunday night; television reporter **Bill Welsh** at left.

handsome devil. . . . They lifted him up by the harness and began to swing him toward the pit opening. Tommy Francis tried to grab one of McCulloch's feet so he could guide the doctor into the shaft.

Most likely because of his claustrophobia, McCulloch began to protest, to fight. He was up in the air, above the pipe, when the crane operator lowered him to Bill Yancey's level. McCulloch was in the throes of a panic attack, raving. According to Tommy Francis, Yancey punched the doctor and knocked him senseless, and they lowered him down as he slowly came to his wits. He then

Kathy's body shrouded from view.
Opposite: Bill Yancey lowers Kathy's body, wrapped in a blanket, late on Sunday night.

encountered Kathy—probably at the edge of the tunnel and the Johnson Well. He determined that she was dead.

Dr. Hanson told Dave and Alice Fiscus the news inside their home. Bill Welsh later claimed that he was asked by the police to bring the news to the small white cottage, but Kathy's parents already knew. "They lived about a block away," Welsh recalled, "and I walked over to the house and knocked. There was no television there. Just the family and me. They let me in and I said, 'I'm very sorry to have to tell you that Kathy is not coming back.'"

Back at the site, Bill Yancey went down again. Kathy's body was wedged tightly in the old well casing. Somehow, Bill Yancey changed her into a dry romper and wrapped her body in a blanket. She was slowly brought out of the well and into the rescue shaft. Then she was lifted to the surface by ropes. Yancey coached those up above. "Keep it coming up gently. Easy, men. Easy."

Though the rescuers had known for several hours that little Kathy was dead, the crowd did not hear the news until nearly 8:53 p.m., when Dr. Hanson made an announcement: "Ladies and gentlemen, Kathy is dead and has apparently been dead since she was last heard speaking Friday."[4] Hanson relayed the family's thanks to the rescuers. "There is nothing we can say to thank the people who helped by their many sacrifices," he said. He then asked the crowd to disassemble and depart. "If this had been your child," he said, "we are sure you would not want a crowd remaining at the scene of the tragedy."[5]

Reporter Stan Chambers signed off for KTLA:

And now it is nine o'clock Sunday night, probably the longest television broadcast in history. And we're sorry that this is the way we have to sign off, because we always hoped that we would have had a happy ending. We want to thank you for staying with us during these long, long hours, and for being with us. I know the family feels the same way, and appreciates the sorrow as you've expressed. And so, ladies and gentlemen, we leave San Marino . . . hoping to have given you the service that we wanted to. And now we return you to our studio.[6]

Sometime around 10:00 p.m., Bill Yancey appeared at the top of the rescue shaft with the body of the little girl. Photographer Leigh Wiener later said that it was as if 350 photographers clicked their shutters at exactly the same moment. A hearse, not one of the waiting ambulances, took Kathy's body to St. Luke's Hospital.

Back in the offices of the Associated Press, Wiener's boss ordered him to go home and get some sleep. "Incidentally," he said, "your picture of the kid's swing has run in over a hundred papers throughout the world."[7]

Throughout the next many hours, as if motivated by vengeance, heavy machinery crumpled up the old Johnson Well casing. The dozers and diggers bent the metal tube over on itself. The well and the two parallel rescue shafts were covered up and buried twenty feet below the earth, and the field returned to its "dusty barrenness."[8] Raymond Hill said that when they finished the cleanup, all anyone would think of the field is that it had recently seen some plowing.

At least one news report demurred, saying instead that the cleanup had left "a mound of dirt . . . like a freshly dug grave."[9]

Chapter 13

ON TUESDAY, APRIL 12, the *Los Angeles Times* published a statement from the Fiscus family:

> We will never be able to adequately thank our friends, both close at home and all over our great American country, for their wonderful help and assistance, their good wishes and their messages of sympathy at this so trying time. From the hundreds of telegrams which we have received and from the thousands of telephone calls which have been directed to our attention, we feel that some of our friends wish to send flowers. We appreciate this very much, but flowers last such a short time. If an equivalent amount of money were sent to the Children's Hospital in Los Angeles, a nonprofit, nondenominational hospital caring only for children, we feel that our little Kathy's untimely death might be the cause of saving some child for a useful life. We sincerely hope this will be the outcome and we will be informed in each and every case.[1]

The day before, Randal Dickey, the state assembly member who ran the committee that had just recently heard David Fiscus testify about old wells, called for the legislative body to adjourn "out of respect to the memory of the late Kathy Fiscus."[2] It was

Dickey who had called Dave Fiscus to testify about the dangers posed by old wells. Chaplain Torrance Phelps offered a prayer to open the proceedings of the State Assembly following the adjournment of the previous day:

> We pray this morning for the children who are present. For the innocence and joy of all children who fill our homes with light and happiness. We rejoice in their bright hopes and the ambition to make America the Paradise for childhood, where every youthful dream can be fulfilled. We pray that parents may be able to provide their young with homes of beauty and with the interests that will make home that enduring attraction that never loses its charm. May we as guardians of their destiny do our utmost to assure them of a world free from fear and want and war.[3]

At the request of one of the members, the assembly ordered "Ode to Kathy Fiscus" to be printed in the record:

> O Master, on high, see Thy child below
> Entombed, helpless, in this grasping hold;
> ·Holy Christians, toiling at life's release
> The love of fellow-man shall now increase.
> O California, hail thy heroes souls
> More precious that your stately mountains gold;
> Promote not wealth or earthy vanity
> Ever hold high this loving humanity.
> O America, to valiant hearts in faith
> On Palm Sunday, grant thine own kindly grace;
> O Savior, Thy servants emulate well

To merit life eternal, with Thee dwell.
O World, turn thy eyes to San Marino
See this devotion mankind here bestows;
Now shines like stars and beaming sun above
Glow for God and Kathy in Divine Love.[4]

On Wednesday, the Fiscus family held the funeral for their Kathy at the Little Stone Chapel attached to a mortuary in Alhambra, the small town just south of San Marino. Kathy was dressed in her frilly white Easter dress, holding Calico, her favorite doll, and lying in a plush blue casket. At the funeral, attended by three hundred mourners in the church and as many as a thousand outside of it, the services were piped outside by a public address system. An Irish lullaby was played, one that Alice often sang to Kathy. It was her favorite song.

Kathy's casket was open. For hours preceding the service, the crowd passed silently by. The press reported that she looked as though she was sleeping peacefully, freed now from her terrible ordeal several days earlier. Actor Lionel Barrymore sent a five-foot, white-rose-and-sweet-pea floral arrangement in the shape of a cross. The actor, who had lost both his daughters in their infancy, sent a card with the flowers: "Deepest sympathy, Lionel Barrymore."

Many of the rescue workers attended the service, and photographers made sure to get pictures of them dressed in their funeral best. Her burial followed in Chula Vista. Kathy's grave marker reads, "One little girl who united the world for a moment." David Fiscus's boss with California Water & Telephone commissioned artist Katherine Skeele Dann to paint an oil portrait of Kathy from photographs as a gift to the family.[5]

Rescue workers at
Kathy's funeral.

Chapter 14

"The wonder of this life is not that one lives to be eighty, but one lives to be eight."
—*Dallas Morning News,* "Kathy," April 12, 1949

HOW DID KATHY FALL into the well in the first place? Maybe she tripped. Maybe she just fell in. Kathy may have been holding hands with the older children as they all ran and played, and when they encountered that old well in the weeds, she slipped down its dark depths. Maybe the kids were playing hide-and-seek. City Engineer Paul Barton said years later that the kids told him Kathy was hiding in the well casing, holding on to the edge of it as her feet dangled below, and she just let go. Given the scant size of the opening, and the fact that the casing may have been above the level of the ground by a few inches, it is hard to imagine Kathy accidentally falling into it—both feet simultaneously, apparently—unless she had imagined it as a place to hide. Perhaps she perched for a moment on its edge and then just tumbled in?

How Kathy Fiscus died remains even more enigmatic. Though an autopsy was performed, the record was not preserved. There are several possibilities as to the cause of death. The accepted and quasi-official cause (absent any ability to refer to the autopsy) was asphyxiation, or apoxia. Trapped in a very small space, with her arms and legs pressed hard up against her chest—"jackknifed," as one report said—Kathy is presumed to have drifted off into unconsciousness fairly quickly sometime Friday evening, within an hour or two of falling into the well. The theory assumes that she simply died in the tight space. No bones were broken, though she did have abrasions on the right side of her body from the fall down the well.[1]

Another idea, one hard to contemplate, is that the rope lowered down to her wrapped around her neck and, when it was pulled from the top, strangled her. That could have happened, and apparently some of the rescuers believed it did.[2] The first responders did not spend much time on this attempt precisely because they feared lassoing Kathy around her neck. When they threw the rope into the Johnson Well after abandoning this approach, they might have done so because they feared that the loop had gone round her neck. If so, it was just too dangerous either to pull her up or let her slide further down with the rope secured up top.

Kathy may have drowned. She probably did. Many of the rescue workers commented on how wet Kathy was when she was found. When they opened the first window into the well above her, water rushed out. Orpheus Kelly told a reporter that he "knew she was dead the minute I saw her. She was three feet below the level of the window in the well casing. She was upright and covered with water."[3]

Given all the water that was in the tunnel, the well had tapped into the water table of the Raymond Basin. Though Kathy fell mostly dry down that long pipe, she had encountered water at the point where she stopped. Enough water to cause her death by drowning? The *New York Times* reported Kelly's comment that she was found "upright and covered with water," and Bill Yancey said that "there'd been water, lots of water" in the pipe when he found her. Newspaper reports said that her hands and feet were macerated, softened by having soaked so long in water.[4]

The contemporary comments and later recollections of Dr. Paul Hanson, the Fiscus family physician, are the most mysterious. At the site on Sunday evening, he told several people (Kathy's aunt among them) that Kathy had drowned.[5] More than thirty years later, the story became more complicated. In 1980, Hanson told interviewer Rick Castberg that, when discovered, Kathy "was in water, had drowned." After noting that the physician who performed the autopsy (Hanson attended but did not lead the effort) was an amateur—"this guy had no idea what the hell he was doing"—Hanson added that "her lungs were full of water." But within moments, he unaccountably switched gears. "No, pardon me; her lungs were not full of water," he said. "Which proved that she had not drowned." Instead, Hanson insisted that Kathy's "chest had been compressed, by this pipe, as she slid into it. So she died of suffocation [because] she couldn't breathe."

But—again according to Hanson—the physician who had performed the poor autopsy had apparently reached a different conclusion. "He said she's drowned, and there was no lung, no water in her lungs." That physician would have been Harry Deutsch of the Los Angeles County Coroner's Office. Back in 1949, Deutsch had given conflicting comments to the press. He told reporters that, while he could not confirm nor deny Hanson and McCulloch's assessment that Kathy had drowned, he certified that the official cause of death was suffocation or asphyxiation. According to Sydney, Australia's *Morning Herald* on April 13, Deutsch made a concerted effort to "say definitely thereby scotching widely heard rumours that she was not strangled by a rope thrown to her in the early minutes of the grim struggle to save her."

In 1980, Dr. Hanson completed the interview with perhaps the most telling recollection, mysterious and awful all at once: "And I felt that people would feel better if she hadn't drowned. And also I made sure there was no coil around her neck. No sign of a rope around her neck, so the poor firemen could be off the hook. But we could see that her . . . ribs were, her cartilages were crushed by the fall. And so there wasn't any question as to what had happened. But the pathologist didn't know this. He said she was drowned."

Hanson apparently took it upon himself to change the record with the coroner. "I called him up," he said, "and I told him what had happened and told him what to look for, and he did. So that it was announced that she had suffocated and not drowned. And she had suffocated immediately. Which she had to have. Because she fell down and she probably had enough force until the thing got narrow and when she did hit [smacks palms] it just [smacks palms] crushed her chest together, you know. So this is how she died."[6]

The world first heard that Kathy had drowned, but after the autopsy, word spread that she had instead suffocated. Story after story suggested that, as her oxygen levels fell or her ability to breathe grew more compromised, Kathy simply drifted off into unconsciousness. We do not know. We will not know. Pressed in 1980 about the cause of death, Dr. Hanson insisted, albeit a bit unsteadily, "Yeah, but what happened . . . she was just suffocated."[7]

People likely did not want to think of the little girl, alive at first, slipping down deeper into the well as the rescue effort went on above her, unable to keep her head above water, drowning ninety feet below. I think Tommy Francis's painful recollection of seeing

Kathy's tear-stained face must be wrong, and that what he saw was not tears but residue from the water that surrounded her until the window was cut. We are not likely to ever know. As rescue worker Paul Barton said, "It's a bad dream, if you know what I mean."[8]

The Fiscus family received thousands of letters from across the world.[9] At the same time, money poured in. Not for the family, as we might expect in our crowdsourced, GoFundMe world; the money was for the rescue workers. Adults sent checks and cash. Children cracked their piggy banks. Donations ranged from pennies

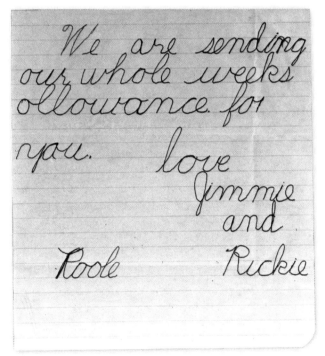

Children sent their savings from their piggy banks to the fund created for the rescue workers.

to hundreds of dollars. One person wrote, "This contribution helps me feel I had a little part in digging that rescue hole."[10]

Tens of thousands of dollars rolled in: $30,000, $40,000, and more. The press reported that people from mining towns were heavily represented among the donors; mining people knew the dangers down below.[11]

What to do with all the money? One plan was to divide it evenly among the workers, but that did not account for the various degrees of danger the rescuers faced during the operation. That plan was laid aside in favor of dividing the money among those workers who had been underground and those who had helped from above ground, excepting the wealthy and the public or law enforcement officials. San Marino officials who supervised the project sought help from Raymond Hill, who came up with a proposal. In a letter to San Marino mayor Clark Bell, the chairman of the Kathy Fiscus Rescue Fund Committee, Hill explained his strategy with care.

Hill wanted to cut through misinformation and the glare of publicity. He believed that some of the rescue workers had been singled out in the press for extravagant praise, while others remained anonymous despite heroism at the scene. His plan distributed units of credit to the men for their work, and it provided extra units for time spent underground. When all the units for all the men were added up, Hill suggested that this number be used to divide the total amount of money, thus fitting the cost per unit (which got pegged at eight dollars). The money was then to be distributed depending on the number of units attributed to each man's work. Hill expected that some of the rescue workers would turn the money down.

Raymond Hill's exacting tabulation is an astonishing thing.

Algorithmic in precision, it includes more than a hundred names. Despite the presence of women at the scene, who also provided volunteer support to the effort, there are no women on Hill's list. Hill saw his calculations as a way to reward those who had placed themselves in harm's way.

Hill and Mayor Bell supervised the distribution of the fund through the summer of 1949. First responders working their jobs—the firemen and policemen on scene, for instance—were not eligible for any money. Rescuer shares ranged from a couple of hundred dollars to over a thousand dollars. Bill Yancey, Don Metz, Whitey Blickensderfer, and Hill received the largest payouts. Hill suggested that some of the men might wish to donate their shares, as he had done, to the Claremont Colleges for memorial scholarships for young women. Twelve of the rescuers agreed to this idea.

But this scholarship plan incensed some of the rescuers and donors, who were quick to take offense at what they said was the elitism of the engineer, his engineering firm, the engineering profession, and the Claremont Colleges all together. The tragedy had brought us together, they insisted, and Hill's plan threatened all of that. The funds earmarked for the college were given to the men first, who could then decide what to do with it once they received it. Clyde Harp bought a new car.[12] One worker used his money to buy a television set for little girls at the Santa Teresita Tuberculosis Sanatorium in Duarte. The girls named their new TV "Kathy."[13]

As time unspooled after the rescue attempt, tragedy dogged many of those who had put themselves in harm's way over that terrible weekend. At the end of 1949, rescuer George Lloyd Green, who operated a crane at the site and helped fill the well and two shafts, was killed at age thirty-seven in a bridge construction accident in Riverside County. Parts of a wayward steel girder, dropped by faulty equipment, swung into him. His family received $60,000 in a wrongful death settlement.

On June 25, 1952, Barbara Belle Hill, wife of Raymond Hill, died in a traffic accident at the quiet residential intersection of Old Mill Road and Oak Knoll Avenue in San Marino, just a mile and a half from the Johnson Well site. Barbara's car collided with another driven by a young woman who lived in the neighborhood. The force of the impact sent Barbara's car out of control, and it smashed into a tree.

A year and a half later, someone murdered rescue worker Orpheus Kelly's wife, Helene, in their Temple City home. Orpheus, who had received a job offer from Howard Hughes only days after the Fiscus rescue attempt, went back and forth between work in Playa Vista and home in Temple City. Helene Kelly, who had been with her husband at the rescue scene throughout the ordeal, was bludgeoned to death by a would-be burglar. The murderer, said to be a male in his teens or twenties by the sound of his voice, called the crime into the sheriff's office. The man, who was never apprehended, had cut the phone and power lines to the house before gaining forced entry. Police officers found Helene in the rear of the home and said she told them an intruder had broken into the house. "Help me, help me. Oh, my head," she said, before lapsing into unconsciousness.[14] Though a suspect at first, Orpheus was not charged.

In April 1958, only a block from where Barbara Hill died in the 1952 car wreck, fate called for Bill Yancey. Ignoring precautions about the sewer-pipe ditch he was digging—which had not been property shored up—Yancey climbed inside and the sides collapsed atop him. Lloyd Van Buskirk of the Pasadena Fire Department, who had arrived early to the scene of the Kathy Fiscus rescue in the department's new rig, remembered that he "dug up [Yancey] dead. He didn't even have a chance to bend over. He was still standing with the shovel."[15]

Whitey Blickensderfer fell into his own dark space, dead from alcohol abuse not many years after the rescue attempt. Cancer took Klaus Landsberg at age forty in 1956, robbing American media of one of its most ingenious innovators. Within weeks of the Kathy Fiscus event, country music artist Jimmie Osborne recorded a song called "The Death of Little Kathy Fiscus." The 78-rpm record sold more than a million copies and became a top ten hit. Others covered it in later years. Osborne shot himself to death at thirty-five in 1958.

Some might think of all this collateral death and damage as a kind of jinx. Just as King Tut presumably aimed his curse at those who dared disturb his tomb and rest, tragedy seems to have stalked so many of those who had tried to rescue Kathy Fiscus. One can understand trying to make some sense out of all this, even if wildly speculative and mythic sense. "Oh, I'm telling you," Tommy Francis said more than thirty years after the event, "the eleven men that actually was in on this, the top eleven men, some of the tragedy. Some of the tragedy . . ."[16] If only he were around today to be asked what he meant by that ominous, cryptic sentence, which conspicuously trails off.

It seems more likely that tragedy sadly coincides with the unalloyed danger of what men like Bill Yancey did for a living. All those genealogies of time and distance converging at the site of the old Johnson Well in the spring of 1949, and then radiating outward from it once the awful event had concluded. Some would die sooner than others; some would wrestle with more and bigger demons than others.

⚬

The modest Fiscus home overlooking the field at 2590 Robles Avenue was torn down a few years after 1949, and the Fiscus family moved around the corner to the house at 2570 Wallingford Road, which is still there. They could probably still see the field from their back windows. The house is located against the old reservoir that shows up in the aerial photography of the rescue effort. Trees now block the view to where the old Johnson Well once was.

Following their move, Dave Fiscus superintended some work or improvements near where the old Johnson Well lay broken and buried. One cannot imagine how hard that must have been on him, wandering once again in that field of grief.[17] Years afterward, a sinkhole briefly opened at the old well site before it was quickly filled in.

Pillars of the San Marino community, Dave and Alice Fiscus stayed active in social, church, and charitable circles.

Alice, who kept a small box of memorabilia tied to the rescue attempt, kept in touch with some of the workers over the years.

Kathy's big sister Barbara remembers that her parents protected her with a fierce vigilance after April 1949. They never spoke of the event—"never again"—though when Barbara would say to friends and others that she was an only child, her mother would become furious. To this day, Barbara occasionally brings flowers to her baby sister's grave.[18] Cousin Gus Lyon apparently never spoke of the day, either. When reached by phone, he said that the kids were playing hide-and-seek in the field and that Kathy may have perched on the edge of the well and just fell in.

Alice Fiscus did not speak easily or often about Kathy. The unusual surname would occasionally cause people to remark on Kathy, whereupon Alice would "very quietly say [she] was Kathy's mother."[19] People would drive to the neighborhood to try to figure out where the Johnson Well was located, and Alice remembers that unknown visitors would place flowers on Kathy's grave in Chula Vista.

In the spring of 1957, a boy named Benjamin Hooper fell down a well in his backyard in rural New York. When he was saved, reporters sought out Alice Fiscus for comment. "We are very thankful," she said, "that they got the boy out, and got him out as quickly as they did."

The Fiscus family moved north to Monterey in 1968. Friends and neighbors threw them a big going-away dinner at the nearby Huntington-Sheraton Hotel. Carver Elementary School went away, too (a new one with the same name was built nearby, on the other side of Huntington Drive). San Marino High School was built in its place in 1955; what remains of the old Johnson Well sits beneath a lane of the track that goes around the football field, at the western end zone.

In April 1999, the San Marino Rotary Club placed a plaque near where the Fiscus home had once been. "For Kathy," it said. "Fifty years ago today, the miracles of radio and television transported our entire nation to this field. Here we witnessed the courageous attempt of so many to save the life of a little girl named Kathy Fiscus. This should not be a spot to recall sadness, this should be a place to visit and say prayers."

Leigh Wiener returned to the site of the rescue
attempt a year later. He took this picture of the
broken swing at the Fiscus home.

Chapter 15

PHOTOGRAPHS OF THE Kathy Fiscus rescue attempt—especially Leigh Wiener's image of the empty swing and another (by a different photographer) of the rescue scene captioned "Please God Help Us Find Her"—became famous nationwide. Polled at the end of 1949, editors of world newspapers picked the Kathy Fiscus story as the sixth biggest story of the year. Number one was the announcement of a Soviet nuclear test; number two centered on the Communist takeover in China.[1]

Kathy Fiscus reverberated, and still reverberates, through American culture. Billy Wilder's unrelentingly dark 1951 film, *Ace in the Hole,* is drawn in part from the Fiscus story, although it is more directly influenced by the sad tale of Floyd Collins, a spelunker who died while trapped in a Kentucky cave in 1927. The film critiqued the carnival-like atmosphere at the scene of both failed rescues.

The same year that Wilder's film was released, a television movie named *The Well* also premiered. It adapted the Kathy Fiscus story to one directly about race; it was, the *Los Angeles Times* later noted, "the black version of the Kathy Fiscus story." At the film's opening, an African American girl named Carolyn slips into an uncapped well. The film is largely focused on the rescue effort, and ends up as a poignant story of heroism and success, with the town united behind the successful effort to save the little girl. At the conclusion, Carolyn is brought up alive from the depths in a bundle and carried off in an ambulance.[2]

Kathy Fiscus clearly had an effect on Billy Wilder as he wrote and directed the controversial 1964 film *Kiss Me, Stupid*. The movie has a critical scene in which the townspeople gather in front of an appliance store to watch the televisions arrayed there, all playing the same show (featuring Dean Martin singing). Wilder surely got that image from the long Palm Sunday weekend fifteen years earlier.[3]

Dragnet star Jack Webb made a 1959 movie called -30- that dramatizes newspaper life in Los Angeles, and is in part wrapped around the loss of a little girl in a flooded storm sewer. Artist Ed Kienholz made a collage piece, *Ode to Kathy Fiscus* and *A Box for Kathy,* in 1962.[4] Woody Allen's 1987 film *Radio Days* features a radio show backdrop monitoring the attempts to rescue a little Polly Phelps from the well in which she is trapped. A 1992 episode of *The Simpsons* referenced the event when Bart pretends to get trapped in a well.[5]

People tend to think that the iconic image or tale of a child trapped in a well came from the popular television show *Lassie*. But that never happened. There is no episode that includes, "What, Lassie? Timmy's fallen down a well?" Rather, the reference is surely a reverberation of the Kathy Fiscus story in popular culture and imagination.

In the fall of 1987, toddler Jessica McClure tumbled into an abandoned well in Midland, Texas. A fervent rescue operation was immediately launched, and the little girl survived. Reporters again managed to find Alice Fiscus who, in later years, had moved back to northern San Diego County. "You try to forget, each time something like this happens," she said. Offering love and prayers to the McClure family as the rescue operation proceeded, Alice continued, "It's something that's helped us—to think it has helped other children. We had prayers from everywhere in the world. It was absolutely unbelievable." She urged parents to be vigilant about the safety of their children. "Please look in your yard," she said. "Look around where your children play. There was absolutely no way we could have ever seen where Kathy fell."[6]

In the fall of 2009, a helium balloon made to look like a flying saucer floated above Fort Collins, Colorado. Richard and Mayumi Heene claimed that their six-year-old son, Falcon, was inside, in a twisted attempt to gain sympathy and fame. The balloon soared several miles above the small city, and the event attracted worldwide attention. Falcon Heene became "The Balloon Boy," as the world turned its attention to his fate. But he was not aboard the balloon. He was hiding at home. The boy's parents eventually pleaded guilty to crimes over the hoax, and the father spent some time in jail.

As journalists looked for comparisons and history lessons to include in their articles, Kathy's fate and Kathy's story came up once again. However, despite attempts to somehow weave the Heene and Fiscus stories together, the events could hardly have been more different. One was accidental, one deliberate. One child lost, one never in danger. One father pacing near the mouth of an old well in hopeless anxiety, another father culpable, venal, and cruel.

The miraculous rescue of a Thai boys' soccer team from a flooded cave in the summer of 2018 carried Kathy Fiscus back into the news. This will happen again and again; whenever a child is endangered, Kathy Fiscus will be conjured once again.

Epilogue

WHAT IS A HISTORIAN to make of the Kathy Fiscus story? A little girl lost in an instant of play, laughing and shouting with her sister, her cousins, and her little dog. Then, a terrifying fall and a dark, frightening death deep below the surface of the earth as thousands prayed and wept.

When I first began to learn about the event, I thought of the ninety feet that Kathy fell down the Johnson Well. She fell the distance from home plate to first base, or from first to second, or second to third. She would never get home.

I believe that the tragedy brought people together, literally and figuratively, as they held their breath side by side, or across miles, in the shared hope that this little girl would be rescued. A rosebush and plaque placed outside the San Marino Public Library in 1969 makes this hope into a succinct observation: "A Pink Rose to Kathy Fiscus – A Little Girl Who Brought the World Together—For A Moment."

The theme of "the everyday American hero" runs through accounts of the event. It comes across wishful, but the leveling of social class is all over the event coverage. Reports highlight the rescuers as everyday heroes, many of them recent veterans of the Second World War, patriots abroad and now patriots at home. California Congressman Donald Jackson insisted that the Kathy

Fiscus tragedy was "proof that in an hour of trouble, our industry and labor become one unit." Patriotism, selfless sacrifice, and goodness beyond social station, restoration of faith in the nation: it is all here in the story."[1]

"I'm no hero," one of the rescuers said. "It was just a matter of simple humanity." On the contrary. This was an event marked by utter heroism. But that, and the tragic sentimentality and pathos of the event, may obscure other perspectives that we ought to ponder.

The fate of Kathy Fiscus was reported on the front pages of newspapers all over the country. These stories appeared alongside news of the Cold War, with the inevitable invective about Reds, Soviets, and Communists. Following the event's sad conclusion, the *New York Times* editorialized that "we still know, even if the mad theorists at the other side of the world do not, that one life—one tiny life—is beyond price."[2] This makes me cringe: Kathy Fiscus, if not part of the Cold War herself, was made a martyr to it.

To be sure, people wanted to believe something good could come from tragedy. They sent money to the rescuers. Some insisted that the well site be made into a park. Others lobbied for safety regulations aimed at old wells, septic tanks, or sewers. This effort extended even to decorative fishponds, as a little girl had died in one in Santa Monica the very day that Kathy Fiscus had fallen down the Johnson Well. Alice Fiscus later said that the only way she could wrestle with the loss of her daughter was that Kathy's death had saved many children's lives thanks to the various safety laws immediately enacted after her death. Often called "Kathy Fiscus Laws," such regulations and measures soon went into effect across the nation.[3] Parents thought of Kathy and kept vigilant eyes on their children.[4]

Unsurprisingly, Kathy Fiscus became identified with the Cold War complexities of race in America just as soon as she tumbled into the well. Blond-haired and blue-eyed, she became for many in the nation and the press "our little blond angel." In covering the event while it unfolded, the press often pointed to earlier episodes, where a child here or there had been rescued. It is at least curious that the rescuers were often Black, their race called out in the articles as was the custom of the day. The grammar, nomenclature, and punctuation follow a depressing formula of requisite racial identification: a child is rescued following a similar ordeal, the rescue is performed by so and so, comma, "a Negro." At the same time they reported on the moment-by-moment progress of the Fiscus rescue, papers also recalled a much earlier event that had ended happily. Elbert Gray, "a Dallas Negro," entered a "sixty-four-foot well only twelve inches wide to rescue a white boy." Found by the press during the Fiscus rescue attempt, Gray commented that the same thing should have been tried to save Kathy.[5]

The event itself moves in and out of focus. At one moment, it echoes across the national and global contexts of race and class during the Cold War. In the next, the focus is on that old well and what happened at and in it. I think of Alice Fiscus, still grateful years and years later that Kathy had jumped into her arms on that Friday afternoon at Union Station. I think of the Reverend Bernard Crist from the nearby Congregational Church, the man who baptized and buried Kathy. Reverend Crist carefully saved newspaper clippings of the story. His son gave them to me sixty years later. So, too, with rescuer Herb Herpel, heartbroken that he could not save Kathy; his daughter sent me a box full of newspaper clippings that her mother had saved. Herpel "did not talk much about the event," his widow said to me nearly seventy years later. It was probably Herb Herpel who, as the rescue effort dragged on, turned to a reporter at the scene and said, "I've got a kid of my own. I almost feel as if it were my own down there."[6]

I think of the sad ironies splayed across the frenetic newspaper coverage of the event: Kathy's uncertain fate discussed in, for instance, a *Los Angeles Times* piece right next to an advertisement showing a delighted little pigtailed girl. "Am I ever happy!" she exclaims. "My Daddy gave me a brand new Kimball Consolette for my birthday!"

I feel a kindred spirit in Leigh Wiener. We share a fixation with the tragedy. A year after Kathy died, he went out to San Marino and re-photographed Kathy's swing, broken and bedraggled in the Fiscus yard. I wonder if Alice saw him that day. Or Barbara? Then he returned, two years later, taking pictures of the well site and the debris still cast about here and there. What made him do that, I wonder?

It is hard to shake the febrile strangeness of the whole affair: a circus performer or two show up; a mother brings her son or daughter to the old well's lip and offers up the child (or down) as a would-be rescuer; a little person in a full bellhop getup arrives as a candidate for head-first delivery down the well. And the Fiscus family physician turns to others at the scene and says, "My gosh, you're going to kill a midget."[7]

The whole thing was a circus. A circus of worry, confusion, and desperation, still palpable all these many years later. Workers squabbling in unfiltered profanity about the best way to get to Kathy; engineers with expensive equipment jousting with cesspool diggers and Seabee veterans, men who knew how to "throw a lot of dirt."

In the 1940s, 334,313 baby girls born in America were christened Catherine, Kathy, Kathleen, Katherine, or Kathryn. Kathryn Anne Fiscus was of course one of those babies. In the 1950s, that number of all those Katherines, Cathys, and Kathys nearly doubled to 609,559.

As powerful and moving as this is, we have to be careful with interpretation and possible meaning. The 1950s saw the biggest spike in the fertility of American women in United States history. There were a lot more baby girls in the 1950s than in the 1940s. The baby boom was roaring, and all those babies needed names.

But think again of that little girl at the center of our story, that toddler trapped and doomed. Kathy Fiscus represented the baby boom in so many ways that popular culture celebrated: blonde, blue-eyed, Californian, born in 1945 as World War II closed. Nearly 35,000 little girls were named Kathy across the decade of the 1940s. That made that name the eighty-eighth most popular choice for a little girl in 1940s America.

Think now of the 157,914 baby girls named Kathy who were born in the 1950s. In just a few years, as the 1940s gave way to the 1950s, the name skyrocketed in popularity. It became the twenty-second most-popular name for girls in the United States. That is remarkable. No other name moved upwards in anything like that prodigious leap. Kathy Fiscus was Kathryn, of course, but the world knew her as Kathy. People were naming their baby girls for Kathy Fiscus.[8]

Alice Fiscus knew all about these baby girls named after her own. "Many years after the occasion [such a heartbreaking word by which to reference the tragedy], for many years . . . we would get letters from mothers saying, 'I have just had a daughter and I have named her Kathy after you.'"

Could we imagine, could we believe, that those little girls may have been loved and cared for that much more because they had been named for the Kathy who was lost?

I cycle along the residential backstreets of San Marino, north of Huntington Drive—Robles, Wallingford, Santa Anita, Winston—and I think of Kathy Fiscus every single time. I have been to where that field and that well once were, twenty times or more.

My children are tired of me talking about Kathy Fiscus. My daughter and I have walked where the Fiscus house once stood. When my son John was a toddler, I would strap him into the kiddie seat on the back of my bicycle, and we would ride over to San Marino High School. We just drove over to the Fiscus home on Wallingford Road, the one they moved to after they lost their little girl. We parked, and I looked over toward the field. There, beneath what is now a running lane of the track going around the football field, the Johnson Well once dropped hundreds and hundreds of feet into the earth. It is gone now, covered up and destroyed. Miguel Blanco's adobe still sits nearby. The pump house that David Fiscus ordered into service during the rescue attempt is still there.

I see a wash or a ravine in my neighborhood, and I think of Kathy Fiscus. I see the silly flourish of an ornamental wishing well in a front yard, and I think of Kathy Fiscus. I see the new irrigation well recently sunk at the Huntington Library, where I spend half my professional life, and I think of Kathy Fiscus. I hear of tragedy visited upon the smallest, the least, and the most vulnerable among us, and I think of Kathy Fiscus. I look at my two children, and I think of Kathy Fiscus.

I walk the Kathy Fiscus neighborhood. I ride my bike up and down those streets. I have stood out front, conspicuous and nervous, of the home that the Fiscus family later moved into. I doubt many in the neighborhood know anything of what happened near there, on that Palm Sunday weekend a lifetime ago. But if some number of those little girls named for Kathy gained a special measure of devotion, love, and care from their families because of the tragic loss of a single Kathy, is that a meaningful legacy, parallel to the pain?

Maybe that is reckoning enough. I don't know. What I do know is where the Johnson Well once dropped into the aquifer. I know where the Fiscus house was, and I can stand pretty close to where Alice Fiscus stood in her kitchen on that April afternoon, chitchatting with her sister. The Fiscus house is gone, the window is gone, and the Johnson Well is gone.

Water and memory, and hopefully something else, remain.

Notes

Epigraph

1. From San Marino Historical Society files on Kathy Fiscus. The San Marino Police Department card is later labeled "Fiscus, Katherine. Fatal." Original spelling is "call was recived," which I have corrected. It is not clear who made the call. It may have come from a Los Angeles County Sheriff already at the scene.

Chapter 1

1. Alice Fiscus interview with Rick Castberg, June 10, 1980; author's files.
2. Alice Fiscus interview with Rick Castberg.
3. The Johnson Well was 150 feet west and 800 feet south of the Fiscus home.

Chapter 3

1. The Shorbs hosted many a salon at their home, though one relation complained that the conversations centered mostly on "pipes and reservoirs." The complaint came from "Sue" Wilson's half-sister, Anne. Anne's sister, Ruth, was the mother of famed World War II American general, George Patton Jr. With thanks to https://lacreekfreak.wordpress.com/2010/01/06/an-artesian-belt-in-san-gabriel-part-ii/#more-3273.
2. See San Gabriel Valley Water Co. to William Hertrich, January 14, 1920. Huntington manuscripts, Huntington Library.
3. On casing of the Johnson Well, see "San Gabriel Valley Water Company Annual Statement . . . September 1, 1907 to February 28, 1909," in Henry E. Huntington Papers, HEH mss., 11/6/3. See also Huntington Land and Improvement Company field books related to the San Gabriel Valley Water Company, housed in the Henry E. Huntington Papers, Huntington Library.
4. San Gabriel Valley Water Co., to Frank Griffith, June 5, 1919. Huntington manuscripts, Huntington Library.
5. San Gabriel Valley Water Company annual reports to the California

Railroad Commission are housed in the California State Archives. See, especially, *Annual Report of the San Gabriel Valley Water Company to the Railroad Commission of California for the Year ending December 31, 1916* (Sacramento: California Railroad Commission), and for the year 1919.

Chapter 5

1. Some think a worker cutting back weeds took the cover off so he could drive his weed-cutting tractor around the field, and never put it back on. Some say that the local children knew of the uncapped well and would throw things down it. If that is true, the well would have been uncapped or uncovered for some time.
2. Alice Fiscus interview with Rick Castberg.
3. Terry Anzur, "Everyone's Child: The Kathy Fiscus story as a defining event in local television news," paper in author's files. Author's thanks to Ms. Anzur.
4. Anzur, "Everyone's Child: The Kathy Fiscus story as a defining event in local television news."
5. Gus Lyon phone interview with author, June 2, 2011.
6. This is at least a little in doubt. The California Water & Telephone Company had managed the field, but it seems likely that the property had been recently sold to the Masonic Order. The *Los Angeles Times* reported this on April 10, 1949. If it took place, that transfer of property would have happened not long before Kathy fell into the Johnson Well.
7. "Americana: The Importance of One Little Girl." *Newsweek*, April 18, 1949. The *Los Angeles Times* of April 10, 1949, reported that David Fiscus had returned to San Marino the very afternoon that Kathy fell into the well. "Friday afternoon, only a few hours before his daughter tumbled into a San Marino well shaft, he had arrived from Sacramento." His testimony took place before the famed "Dickey Committee," an early state investigation into ground and air pollution and the dangers posed to public health; the committee sought expert testimony from, among others, "representatives of the water well drilling profession." David Fiscus would have testified on April 6 or 7 (or on both days). No hearing was held on April 8. The official name of the committee, chaired by State Assemblyman Randal F. Dickey, was the "Assembly Interim Committee on Water Pollution and Industrial Wastes." The document that the committee produced, likely with the assistance of David Fiscus's testimony, is "Preliminary Report, Assembly Interim Committee on Air and Water Pollution," (Sacramento: Assembly of the State of California, 1951). My thanks to Robert Pierotti for the reference. David Fiscus's testimony is not preserved in the record.

8. Anzur, "Everyone's Child: The Kathy Fiscus story as a defining event in local television news." It is not clear from the record if David Fiscus's company still owned the field. It certainly had once owned it, as it had purchased the Western Utilities Corporation holdings, which included the Johnson Well. But sale to the "San Marino Foundation," the outfit that considered building a Masonic Temple on the site, may have taken place by April 1949.

9. Lloyd Van Buskirk interview with Rick Castberg, June 30, 1980; author's files.

10. Dr. Paul Hanson, the obstetrician who had attended Kathy's birth and delivered her by Caesarean section, said later that "the firemen were afraid that they may have gotten this rope around her neck and strangled her, and they were really worried." Dr. Paul Hanson interview with Rick Castberg, July 2, 1980; author's files.

11. Lloyd Van Buskirk interview with Rick Castberg; author's files.

12. Quoted in Anzur, "Everyone' Child: The Kathy Fiscus story as a defining event in local television news."

13. Tommy Francis interview with Rick Castberg, July 7, 1980; author's files. Francis said he heard about the accident from the motorcycle officer. Documentation he filed after the failed rescue event that outlined the hours he worked at the site, said he first heard about Kathy from "an anonimous [sic] phone call received by me at 6:00 p.m., Friday evening April 8, 1949." Memo to Chief of Police Glenn McClung from Tommy Francis, April 19, 1949; copy in author's files.

Chapter 6

1. 1900 U.S. Census. The wording regarding Howard's occupation is difficult to decipher, but the word "mule" can be made out—it's possible that he was a mule tender.

2. 1910 U.S. Census.

3. 1920 U.S. Census.

4. WWI Draft Registration Card, 12 Sep 1918; 1930 U.S. Census.

5. 1900 U.S. Census [listed on Ancestry.com as "J Horner Fiscus"].

6. 1910 U.S. Census lists Fiscuses as being married for three years; 1930 U.S. Census lists his age at marriage as twenty-eight and his wife's age at marriage as twenty-three.

7. 1910 U.S. Census [listed on Ancestry.com as "J Homer Friers"]; WWI Draft Registration Card, 12 Sep 1918.

8. 1920 U.S. Census [listed as "Homer Fiscus"].

9. 1930 U.S. Census.

10. 1900 U.S. Census lists "Elizabeth F. Loveland"; 1910 U.S. Census lists "Elizabeth Fiscus"; 1920 U.S. Census lists "Florence E. Fiscus" living with her husband Homer Fiscus, mother-in-law Catherine Loveland, and children David H. and Elizabeth L. Fiscus—perhaps after her daughter's birth she began using Florence as her first name; 1930 U.S. Census lists "Elizabeth L. Fiscus"—presumably she began using Loveland as her middle name after marriage, though this may cause some confusion since she also has a daughter named "Elizabeth L. Fiscus." Elizabeth died in October 1957; California Death Index.

11. 1920 U.S. Census.

12. 1930 U.S. Census.

13. From California Water & Telephone newspaper history file, Water Resources Collections and Archives, University of California, Riverside.

14. 1905 Minnesota State Census.

15. U.S. General Land Office Records, Homestead Entry, 30 Jun 1884.

16. Minneapolis City Directories, 1890, 1891; the 1905 Minnesota State Census recorded that Chester and his wife had lived in that census district for fifteen years, suggesting that he arrived in Hennepin County just before the 1890 city directory listing.

17. 1905 Minnesota State Census.

18. Minnesota Death Index.

19. WWI Draft Registration Form C (12 Sep 1918); incorrectly listed as "Kinmone" on Ancestry.com for 1920 Census; 1905 Minnesota State Census; California Death Index.

20. 1905 Minnesota State Census.

21. WWI Draft Registration Form C (12 Sep 1918). Thanks to my friend, historian Peter Neushul, for his help on the plant and on the science of turning kelp to munitions.

22. 1920 U.S. Census.

23. Obituary of Alice M. Fiscus, *Pomerado News*, June 12, 2008.

24. California Birth Index; U.S. Social Security Death Index; Obituary of Alice M. Fiscus, *Pomerado News*.

25. Obituary of Alice M. Fiscus, *Pomerado News*.

26. Mrs. Bruce Stephens, whose husband worked with David Fiscus at the California Water & Telephone Company, told me (phone interview, May 21, 2017) that Dave Fiscus had an uncle who was a prominent executive with the company, and that he "owned it." This would have been Chester Loveland, a name brought to my attention by Kathy Fiscus's big sister, Barbara, in a phone conversation on January 30, 2018. Chester Loveland

would have been David Fiscus's mother's brother, and his prominence in the water company went back to the old Sweetwater days. He had been the chief hydraulic engineer of the California Railroad Commission before starting his own firm. At one point, he was chairman of the board and president of the West Coast Telephone Company, the California Water & Telephone Company, and the Southwestern States Telephone Company.

27. "Americana: The Importance of One Little Girl." *Newsweek*, April 18, 1949 refers to David Fiscus as the "regional manager." Correspondence in 1965 indicates that he was manager of the "San Gabriel Valley Division," and had been so since the very early 1940s.

Chapter 7

1. *Los Angeles Times*, April 10, 1949.
2. From Paul Barton interview. "I . . . called my superintendent and had all the city employees of the street department come in and we barricaded streets trying to keep the public out."
3. *Los Angeles Times*, April 10, 1949.
4. At least one rescue worker who had digging and/or cesspool experience told me that this was entirely unnecessary given that the well was open at one end, though admittedly far from where Kathy was lodged.
5. Anzur, "Everyone's Child: The Kathy Fiscus story as a defining event in local television news."
6. Tommy Francis disputed this. He claimed that he could hear Kathy for much longer afterwards. But the press coverage says she stopped crying around 6 p.m. Tommy Francis interview with Rick Castberg.
7. For more on Raymond Hill's career, see J. David Rodgers, "Threadlines of Geotechnical and Engineering Geology firms in Southern California," posted at http://web.mst.edu/~rogersda/Geotechnical-Practice.
8. Tommy Francis interview with Rick Castberg.

Chapter 8

1. Tommy Francis interview with Rick Castberg.
2. Barbara Fiscus, telephone interview with author, January 30, 2018.

Chapter 9

1. From unnamed clipping; author's files.
2. *Pasadena Star News*, April 10, 1949.
3. *Los Angeles Times*, April 9, 1949.

4. An unnamed clipping in author's files makes the likely apocryphal suggestion that Blickensderfer got his nickname at the site. Arriving at the site to help on Friday night, he was asked by Don Metz what his name was. "Homer E. Blickensderfer," he replied. "Yeah, well, you got light hair, so we'll call you Whitey on this job. Let's go." Blickensderfer was said to have replied, "That's jake with me." As to his hernia condition, Blickensderfer had it surgically repaired, free of charge, in late April 1949. See *Los Angeles Times*, April 22, 1949. Frances Blickensderfer quoted in the *Los Angeles Evening Herald and Express*, April 11, 1949.
5. Author's phone interview with Nancy Herpel, May 16, 2017.
6. Paul Barton interview. In and around the coverage of the event, Yancey was often described as kin to a famous Confederate officer of the same name; but the relationship, if there was one, is murky.
7. See *71st U.S. Naval Construction Battalion* (U.S. Navy Seabee Museum, n.d.). This publication has several photographs of Yancey performing Seabee duty, including minesweeping.
8. Anzur, "Everyone's Child: The Kathy Fiscus story as a defining event in local television news."

Chapter 10

1. Anzur, "Everyone's Child: The Kathy Fiscus story as a defining event in local television news."
2. Television newsman Bill Welsh, who would play a big role in the Fiscus event, later estimated that there were something like 300 televisions in Southern California as World War II ended. See "Bill Welsh Marks 50th Year in Broadcasting," *Los Angeles Times*, June 4, 1985.
3. See, for example, https://www.britishpathe.com/video/a-nation-mourns-for-kathy-fiscus-aka-child-rescue/query/child
4. Anzur, "Everyone's Child: The Kathy Fiscus story as a defining event in local television news."
5. Bill Welsh interview with Rick Castberg, July 16, 1980; author's files.
6. Bill Welsh interview with Rick Castberg.
7. See, also, "Landsberg: TV's Dynamic Pioneer," *Los Angeles Times*, September 16, 1966.
8. Quoted in Anzur, "Everyone's Child: The Kathy Fiscus story as a defining event in local television news." On Landsberg narrating stories from the scene, see "Landsberg: TV's Dynamic Pioneer."
9. Quoted in Anzur, "Everyone's Child: The Kathy Fiscus story as a defining event in local television news." This quote was almost certainly spoken by Raymond Hill.

10. Clyde Harp interview with author, May 12, 2008. There was also concern that the vibrations caused by the big equipment would cause the old well casing to collapse around itself.
11. "What did you look at most of the time? You looked at the end of a pipe, hole in the ground, some people walking around. Some equipment, cranes that could lift things and so forth. And a lot of times you wouldn't see anything. It would be completely static." Bill Welsh interview with Rick Castberg.
12. *Pasadena Star News*, April 10, 1949.
13. *Pasadena Star News*, April 10, 1949. The number of miners at the scene reminds us how prevalent that occupation was, and in some ways continued to be, in the first half of the twentieth century in the far West. It also suggests, as in the case of this miner-turned-sailor, how the occupation had begun to dry up and encourage itinerancy.
14. Bill Welsh interview with Rick Castberg.
15. Bill Welsh interview with Rick Castberg.
16. See *New York Times*, April 10, 1949.

Chapter 11

1. Tommy Francis interview with Rick Castberg.
2. Clyde Harp interview with author, May 12, 2008.
3. Quoted in Anzur, "Everyone's Child: The Kathy Fiscus story as a defining event in local television news."
4. Quoted in Anzur, "Everyone's Child: The Kathy Fiscus story as a defining event in local television news."
5. Tommy Francis interview with Rick Castberg.
6. Some reports claimed that the pumping filled the reservoir nearby and that a second catch basin had to be utilized.
7. Tommy Francis interview with Rick Castberg.
8. *New York Times*, April 11, 1949.
9. *New York Times*, April 11, 1949.
10. Quoted in Anzur, "Everyone's Child: The Kathy Fiscus story as a defining event in local television news."
11. Tommy Francis interview with Rick Castberg.
12. Quoted in Anzur, "Everyone's Child: The Kathy Fiscus story as a defining event in local television news."
13. Clyde Harp: "I was the one who made the first cut into the well casing on my third trip down and found Kathy's body." Whitey Blickensderfer, recovering afterwards in the hospital, said that he had spied Kathy

"crouched up, with her head nestled down on her little shoulder ... I knew right away she was dead." *Los Angeles Times*, April 12, 1949, p. 3. Also Clyde Harp interview with author.

Chapter 12

1. "Television Has 27-Hour 'Fire Trial,'" *Los Angeles Times*, April 11, 1949.
2. Dr. Paul Hanson interview with Rick Castberg.
3. Dr. Paul Hanson interview with Rick Castberg.
4. Quoted in Anzur, "Everyone's Child: The Kathy Fiscus story as a defining event in local television news."
5. "Kathy's Own Doctor Announces Her Death," *Los Angeles Times*, April 11, 1949.
6. Quoted in Anzur, "Everyone's Child: The Kathy Fiscus story as a defining event in local television news."
7. See "A Picture Worth 100 Papers," *Los Angeles Times*, June 20, 1982. See also, "Exhibit Surveys Work of Photojournalist Wiener," *Los Angeles Times*, September 19, 1986.
8. See "Death in Well Laid to Lack of Oxygen," *New York Times*, April 12, 1949.
9. "Kathy Died Quickly and Painlessly, Doctors Think," *Los Angeles Times*, April 12, 1949.

Chapter 13

1. *Los Angeles Times*, April 12, 1949.
2. *California Assembly Daily Journal*, April 11, 1949 (Sacramento: California State Assembly, 1949), p. 1927.
3. *California Assembly Daily Journal*, April 12, 1949 (Sacramento: California State Assembly, 1949), p. 1929.
4. *California Assembly Daily Journal*, April 11, 1949 (Sacramento: California State Assembly, 1949), p. 1940. On receipt of two copies of the poem and of a concurrent resolution of sympathy to the family, David Fiscus later wrote his thanks to the Assembly, noting that he would give one of each to Raymond Hill. "Many thousands of letters of sympathy," he wrote, "have made our sorrow much more easy to bear." David Fiscus to Arthur A. Ohnimus, Chief Clerk, California Assembly, printed in *Assembly Daily Journal*, April 25, 1949, p. 2548.
5. See *Los Angeles Times*, April 13, 1949, p. A8.

Chapter 14

1. The *Los Angeles Times* reported on April 14 that Dave and Alice Fiscus had requested that no inquest be held by the Los Angeles County Coroner's Office.

2. Both Herb Herpel's daughter and widow commented on the wrong-headedness of asking a frightened little girl to somehow get a rope up under her arms while encased in a dark and narrow well. Herpel himself is said to have commented after the rescue attempt that Kathy got "all tangled up in the ropes." Phone interview with Nancy and Nancy (mother and daughter) Herpel, May 16, 2017. Herb Herpel never talked of the rescue attempt. "It really bothered him," his widow remembered. "We had a little girl at home who was the same age as Kathy." The *Los Angeles Times* reported, on April 12th, that the doctors attending the rescue operation said the rope had been entwined around her body and both legs, noting that this was as Kathy had been instructed from the rescuers above ground shortly after she fell on Friday evening. Rick Castberg, conducting an interview with Stan Chambers in 1980, surmised that the rope was around Kathy when she was found: "But I guess when they reached her it was around her." Stan Chambers interview by Rick Castberg, July 3, 1980; author's files.

3. Kelly quoted in the Sydney *Morning Herald,* April 12, 1949.

4. "Child Found Dead, Wedged in Shaft; Died Two Days Ago," *New York Times*, April 11, 1949. See "Exhausted Workers of Rescue Effort Relax After Ordeal," *Los Angeles Times*, April 12, 1949. See also, "Kathy Died Quickly and Painlessly, Doctors Think," *Los Angeles Times*, April 12, 1949.

5. *Los Angeles Times*, April 11, 1949.

6. Hanson interview with Rick Castberg.

7. Hanson interview with Rick Castberg.

8. Paul Barton interview with Rick Castberg, July 1, 1980. In author's files. Barton added that, had the rescue attempt taken place in 1980, Kathy could have been reached in "ten minutes" given the advancement in tools and technology.

9. In the summer of 1950, Barbara Fiscus represented her family as a plaque was dedicated in Kathy's memory at Children's Hospital in Los Angeles. At the ceremony, in which the Fiscus family gave the hospital the nearly $4,000 they had received in the "Fiscus Memorial Fund," David Fiscus noted that the family had been contacted by more than 20,000 people in the aftermath of Kathy's death. See "Sister Unveils Memorial Plaque to Kathy Fiscus," *Los Angeles Times*, August 22, 1950.

10. See, for example, the story of three-and-a-half-year-old Kathy Soderman, who sent two dollars from her piggy bank and promised to send two dollars a week until twenty-five dollars had been given; after receiving Easter gifts, the little girl sent in another six dollars. *Los Angeles Times*, April 13 and April 19, 1949. The average donation hovered around four dollars and fifty cents. Excerpt from letter quoted in *Los Angeles Times*, April 21, 1949.

11. See "Kathy Rescue Fund Donations Pour In," *Los Angeles Times*, April 16, 1949.

12. A partial list of the payouts can be found in "Kathy Fund Checks Sent to 132 Workers," *Los Angeles Times*, May 28, 1949. Clyde Harp received nearly $400. See also, "Names of 111 on Roster for Fiscus Rescue Job," *Los Angeles Times*, May 19, 1949. Tommy Francis said that he and another rescue worker were given $1,000 each in cash by a member of the Doheny family of oil wealth. Though his telling of this is dramatic, it is hard to believe, as Edward Doheny Sr. was dead by 1949. Edward Doheny Jr. was murdered in the family mansion in 1929. Tommy Francis interview with Rick Castberg.

13. The adverse reaction to Hill's scholarship idea can be gleaned from letters to the *Los Angeles Times*, May 13, 1949; one letter writer wrote, "WE WANT EVERY CENT OF THAT MONEY TO GO TO THOSE HEROES." Regarding the television gift, see Anzur, "Everyone's Child: The Kathy Fiscus story as a defining event in local television news," paper in author's files. See also "Kathy Fiscus Worker Donates Television Set," *Los Angeles Times*, July 14, 1949.

14. See "Death of Fiscus Hero's Wife Laid to Unknown," *Los Angeles Times*, November 6, 1953. See also, "Wife of Fiscus Hero Found Clubbed to Death," *Los Angeles Times*, November 1, 1953.

15. Lloyd Van Buskirk interview with Rick Castberg.

16. Tommy Francis interview with Rick Castberg.

17. From email correspondence, October 31, 2011, Garry Hofer, Operations Manager of California American Water (the successor company to the California Water & Telephone Company). A search of Cal American's files "turned up very little, just some old plans for a couple of small improvements that David Fiscus made to the site after the incident." My thanks to Michael Hurley for the introduction to Mr. Hofer.

18. Author's phone interview with Barbara Fiscus.

19. Alice Fiscus interview with Rick Castberg.

Chapter 15

1. Number three was the labor strikes in coal and steel country; four was "high naval officers challenge unification policies"; five was the conviction of eleven "top Communists" in the U.S.; seven was an airplane collision that killed fifty-five people; eight was the treason conviction of a Hungarian count; nine was the marriage of the vice president to a "Missouri widow"; and ten was the tight 1949 pennant race in Major League Baseball. See "Russian Blast Heads Year's 10 Big Stories," *Los Angeles Times*, December 8, 1949.
2. "Black version" line from "Mug Shots," *Los Angeles Times*, October 11, 1981. See Deborah Elizabeth Ramsey, "Caution Children Crossing: Home, Integration Narratives, and the Gentle Warrior, 1950–1965." Ph.D. diss., University of Southern California, 2010.
3. Thanks to Richard Schave for the reference.
4. See https://www.newportbeachindy.com/new-exhibit-draws-on-oc-art-collections/
5. See http://www.popmatters.com/column/118784-the-simpsons-radio-bart-9-january-1992/
6. See *Los Angeles Times*, October 17, 1987. Thinking of Kathy's fate, Clyde Harp reminded me that little Jessica "didn't fall very far." In an eerie reverberation of the dark trouble that chased the Fiscus rescuers, McClure's rescuer, Robert O'Donnell, later took his own life. See the *Los Angeles Times*, May 24, 1995.

Epilogue

1. Jackson quoted in *Evening Vanguard* [Venice, California], April 12, 1949.
2. *New York Times*, April 11, 1949.
3. See, for example, "Kathy Case Causes Action in Oklahoma," *Los Angeles Times*, April 20, 1949, regarding two bills pushing for the sealing of water wells. See also, "Supervisors Pass Well-Capping Law," *Los Angeles Times*, April 20, 1949. In 1957, papers ran a story about an inventor in Texas who, when the Fiscus rescue was being attempted, began work on a device to save the lives of children who fell down wells. It was an odd contraption: an automobile headlight and a fish trap enclosed in a small metal cylinder. Inside the cylinder was a two-way radio, a light, and a little Santa Claus doll. Once the device was lowered in a well, the trapped child would be told to reach for the lighted Santa Claus, at which point looped cords would grab the child's wrist and tighten, and another cord would lasso the child's arm

at the shoulder. The inventor, who said the prototype cost him ten dollars to make, thought it would work in ninety-five percent of cases and that a fully outfitted device would cost about seven hundred dollars. See "Device Built to Rescue Children from Wells," *Los Angeles Times*, May 26, 1957.

4. Raymond Hill's grandson wrote to me that his parents thought about the Kathy Fiscus event as they raised their children. "The first time I heard of it," Gregg Hill wrote me, "was when my dad explained to me why my mom was so paranoid about us 'falling down a well' when we would go play in a field in Sierra Madre or go camping. Even as a young child about eight to twelve years old, I remember them both being *really* adamant about not running around in the desert, not going into open fields, and them saying that there were a lot of open mines and wells just covered with rotting boards that we could fall into and die. I thought they were both nuts until my dad showed me the scrapbook with articles about Kathy Fiscus." Gregg Hill to author, October 26, 2019. In an earlier note, Mr. Hill wrote, "As kids, we would go to the desert and my parents would freak out if we went wandering around, always telling us that there were abandoned wells and mines all over the place. It never dawned on me why they were so fearful." Gregg Hill to author, July 11, 2013.

5. Given the generalized recurrence of "Black rescuer attempting to save white child," one wonders about racialized coercion at such rescue attempts.

6. "My dad was heartbroken that he could not save her," wrote Janice Herpel in an email to the wife of rescue worker Clyde Harp, March 27, 2008; author's copy. See also, *Los Angeles Times*, April 10, 1949, p. 17.

7. Dr. Paul Hanson interview with Rick Castberg.

8. Poet Cathy Smith Bowers, born 1949, the former poet laureate of North Carolina, wrote the poem "Namesake" in memory of Kathy Fiscus. *The Georgia Review* 43, No. 2 (1989): 278–79.

Namesake
for Cathy [sic] Fiscus, 3½, who died in an abandoned well the summer of 1949

From the face of the earth
is how they put it
when someone disappears
so all day your father paces
among bulldozers and cranes
as your mother sits in the car muttering to the visor.

I hang in my own mother's womb,
little turtle, zeppelin of skin and marrow.
The chipped ice she craves grinds in her teeth
like pneumatic saws.

And because television that summer
will be the closest thing to miracle,
she gives in to the sloppy recliner,
to the window fan's rattle and clack
to watch as hour by hour hope fails in black and white.

Down there you must have heard something queer.
A scraping at earth, some ancient burrowing.
And what word can name the descent of midgets
armed with buckets and spades?

You lived two days,
your voice tamping at the surface, that one song
rising now and then into the suspended mike.

Then—air, light. The blood
hammering at the soft closure of my skull, they lifted
me out, all slag and sediment,
of another life,
and gave me your name.

9. Alice Fiscus interview with Rick Castberg. See also https://
wanderingseniors.wordpress.com/tag/kathy-fiscus for a story of one
woman named for Kathy (and two who reply to her story to say that, they,
too, were named for her). A graduate of Burbank High School, class of
1968, noted thirteen Kathys (various spellings) in the class and made the
connection to Kathy Fiscus. See https://burbankhigh1968.net/2012/02/26/
the-story-of-kathy-fiscus-1945-1949. As a macabre aside, a website story
about Kathy Fiscus notes that the author of the story had a sister who
shared Kathy's first and middle name—Kathryn Anne. "From my earliest
days I can recall my parents referring to her as 'little Kathy not in the well,'"
he writes. From http://hiddensandiego.net/Lost-History-Kathy-Fiscus.php.

Acknowledgments

ONE DAY out of the blue, a man named Rick Castberg, retired from the Department of Political Science at the University of Hawaii, got in touch with me. He told me something curious. Based on reading an essay I had written about Kathy Fiscus, he said he thought I was as captivated about the story as he had been at one point in his life years earlier. Rick said he was not going to write the book he had once planned to write. As has happened to all of us, he had moved on to other projects.

He asked if I would like to have his notes and the cassette tapes of the interviews he had done with the family and first responders some thirty years after 1949. I said yes in a heartbeat. Without those, and without that singular act of scholarly and collegial generosity, this book would not exist. Rick and I never got the chance to meet, but he deserves pride of place in these acknowledgments.

When Rick's interviews arrived in a mailer at the Huntington Library, I carried the package gingerly to my office and opened it up. A dozen cassette tapes slid out, thrilling and terrifying me at the same time. At that point, they were already three decades old. I had a tiny, old cassette player, but I did not dare try to use it for fear of ruining the tapes. I left a slightly frantic message for my friend, the multifaceted scholar Josh Kun: *What do I do?* Josh to the rescue; he immediately sent me and the tapes to sound engineer Gary

Hobish in South San Francisco. Gary had no trouble converting the tapes safely to digital format. Now I get to write that I have worked with the same sound engineer who has helped the likes of Willie Nelson, Devo, and Bill Evans. Thank you.

Devik Wiener has been deeply supportive, patient, and kind throughout my years of work on this project. He is a great and loving caretaker of his father's astonishing photographic archive, and I thank him sincerely for his generosity in allowing me to reproduce some of Leigh Wiener's unforgettable images here. Devik understands why and how I feel a kindred spirit to his father.

Jason LaBau helped me with Kathy Fiscus family research; his able and intelligent support is gratefully acknowledged here. So, too, with the superb research support of Annie Heller Salimi. Mike Hart and Michael Hurley guided me through water and well history. Tim Crist shared memories of his father, the Reverend Bertrand Crist, with me. Tim gave me the clippings of the event that his dad had collected and saved. Joyce Schlaker helped transcribe interview files. The late Clyde Harp, one of the men who went deep into the earth in search of Kathy, gave of his time and his memories over the course of several long conversations. Thanks, too, to Sandra Harp. Tanya Carr of the Chula Vista Public Library helped me with genealogical research on the Kinmore family. Diego Ayala helped me find images for this book. Television journalist Terry Anzur shared her deep Kathy Fiscus research with me. My friend Miriam Pawel has been a terrific sounding board for all manner of ideas over the years, including those in this book. Miriam also introduced me to Sam Enriquez of the *Wall Street Journal*. A long, helpful phone call with Sam ensued, and I'm grateful for his creative ideas about narration and storytelling.

Barbara Fiscus and Gus Lyon kindly took my phone calls and answered my questions with grace. Barbara Fiscus Simon sent me family photographs, including the one that is used on the cover of this book, and I will be forever grateful to her. The late Stanley Lyon answered my emails patiently and with care. Thanks to Jeff Burbank for his help in finding Mr. Lyon.

Not long after I first started working on this book, my friend Michael Hurley suggested that I visit the California Department of Water Resources field office in Glendale. It took me years to get around to it, and I almost blew it. When I finally got over there, I met Robert Pierotti. Bob was only a month or so from retirement (or so he said; I have not really seen him retire yet). Had I waited too long, I would have missed one of the most important sources of expertise that helped make this book arrive between hard covers. Bob Pierotti gave of his time and his water well expertise to help me pinpoint the well at the heart of this story, and he painstakingly and expertly read drafts of this book, correcting errors I made in technical arenas and use of nomenclature. It is a pleasure to acknowledge Bob's friendship, his own erudite interest in the Kathy Fiscus story, and his invaluable help to me in telling it.

Craig R. Harvey, chief of coroner investigations for Los Angeles County, helped me track down the registration of Kathy's death ("Suffocation—fell into a 14 inch steel casing—Accidental"). Melissa Chinchillo of the literary agency Fletcher and Company read an early draft of this book on her vacation. Her enthusiasm, patience, and editing suggestions are gratefully acknowledged here. My friend Sam Watters kept an ever-vigilant eye out for well and water history. My thanks to Taryn Haydostian for expert help with images.

Beau MacDonald of Spatial Sciences at USC is as generous as she is brilliant. She helped me find the Johnson Well, and performed geo-spatial magic to put it in time and space. The John Randolph Haynes and Dora Haynes Foundation provided me with a Faculty Fellowship in order to finish this book, and that support is gratefully acknowledged here. I wrote the first draft of this book during a California Writing Residency at the Yefe Nof retreat in the San Bernardino Mountains. What a gift. My thanks to the kind and generous stewards of that place and program. My friend Jonathan Blum has helped me become a better writer. David Igler never let on that he might not like to hear yet another bit of the Fiscus story, and he urged me to get this book done. The same is true for Tom Sitton.

It is a privilege once again to work with Angel City Press. Each step along the way has been a pleasure. Thanks for believing in this unusual project. Terri Accomazzo expertly edited and elegantly reorganized this book and made it so much better. Kate Murray proofread the manuscript with an eagle eye.

To my wife, Jenny, and our children, Helen and John: thank you for your patience with me as I thought long on this event, trying to figure out how to tell the story of it.

About the Photographs

There is a paradox about the images of the rescue attempt and those who took part in it. Across those three days of feverish activity, newsreel images and the live television shots saturated the airwaves. As much as the photographs in this book characterize the event in all its urgency and fear, they were not what most people saw in April 1949. Very few of the images reproduced here actually appeared in print, though some did. What most people saw on that terrible weekend were the filmed scenes brought to life by television and newsreel journalism. While the newsreels can still be viewed (they are compelling), the television footage shot on that Southern California field is not findable nor watchable. We have the photographs. We do not have the television story. Those twenty-four hours of revolutionary on-the-scene reporting no longer exist.

A note on the photographs reproduced here: some come by way of the Los Angeles Times Photographic Archive held at UCLA, and I am especially grateful to Simon Elliott and Genie Guerard for their help. The *Los Angeles Times* allowed me to use additional images from its holdings; thank you to Ralph Drew for all the help. Devik Wiener not only allowed me to use some of his father's remarkable pictures, he scanned them for Angel City Press. Barbara Fiscus Simon sent me a batch of Fiscus family photographs. The one in which she and her younger sister stand together was taken not long before the events of April 1949. Most of the pictures used here came from the late Rick Castberg; he had collected them from various sources over the years, in hopes of someday writing his own book or essay about Kathy Fiscus. When he realized that he was not going to do that, he sent them to me. These pictures do not appear to have been published in 1949; many of them look like variants of photographs that were published. Over the years, people have sent me pictures, and I've gathered others here and there. It's possible that some of these were taken by bystanders in the crowd and that Rick Castberg gathered them up into the picture file he later sent to me at The Huntington. I wish I could track down all these photographs for more detail. But, aside from knowing that they are real, that they bring us to the scene, I have not been able to find out more.

As much as I cherish all these photographs—with a special regard for those taken by then-nineteen-year-old Leigh Wiener—I remain hopeful that a kinescopic reel (a film of a television broadcast) from KTTV or KTLA surfaces someday. It's always best never to say never and to maintain hope.

Unless noted here, photographs in this book are from the collection of Rick Castberg:
- Barbara Fiscus: front cover and 3 (foreground), 13
- *Los Angeles Times*: 66, 125
- UCLA Special Collections, Los Angeles Times Photographic Archive: 66, 125
- Devik Wiener: front cover and 3 (background), 16, 20, 82, 96, 132, back cover (left)

Other Works by William Deverell

Non-Fiction

Shaped by the West: A History of North America, two volumes,
with Anne Hyde

Water and Los Angeles: A Tale of Three Rivers, 1900–1941, with Tom Sitton

Form and Landscape:
Southern California Edison and the Los Angeles Basin, 1940–1990,
co-edited with Greg Hise

Woody Guthrie L.A., 1937–1941, with Darryl Holter

The Blackwell Companion to Los Angeles, co-edited with Greg Hise

The Blackwell Companion to California, co-edited with David Igler

Land of Sunshine: The Environmental History of Metropolitan Los Angeles,
co-edited with Greg Hise

Whitewashed Adobe:
The Rise of Los Angeles and the Remaking of Its Mexican Past

The Blackwell Companion to the American West

Metropolis in the Making: Los Angeles in the 1920s, co-edited with Tom Sitton

Eden by Design: The 1930 Olmsted / Bartholomew Plan for Los Angeles,
with Greg Hise

The West in the History of the Nation, two volumes, with Anne Hyde

Railroad Crossing: Californians and the Railroad, 1850–1910

California Progressivism Revisited, co-edited with Tom Sitton

Fiction

"Driftwood," *The Cost of Paper,* vol. 5, Spring 2018

"Arraigned," *Angels Flight - Literary West,* September 2017

"Evangel" *Exposition Review,* vol. 1, 2016.
Nominated for the PEN/Dau Emerging Writers Award, 2016

About the Author

William Deverell is Director of the Hunting-
ton-USC Institute on California and the West
and Professor of History at the University of
Southern California. He received his under-
graduate degree in American Studies from
Stanford University and his M.A. and Ph.D.
degrees in History from Princeton University.

Kathy Fiscus: A Tragedy that Transfixed the Nation

By William Deverell

Design by Amy Inouye, Future Studio

10 9 8 7 6 5 4 3 2 1

ISBN-13 978-1-62640-087-0

Library of Congress Cataloging-in-Publication Data is available.

Published by Angel City Press
www.angelcitypress.com

Printed in Canada